HELPING YOUR CHILD'S EMOTIONAL GROWTH

HELPING

With an introduction by Milton J. E. Senn, M.D.
DIRECTOR, YALE UNIVERSITY CHILD STUDY CENTER

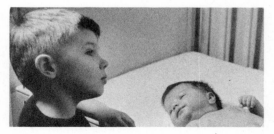

Anna W. M. Wolf and
Suzanne Szasz

YOUR CHILD'S

EMOTIONAL

GROWTH

Doubleday & Company, Inc., Garden City, New York, 1954

DOMINICAN COLLEGE
LIBRARY
SAN RAFAEL

649
W831h

We are grateful to all the mothers who worked with us so generously and patiently on this book; and so we dedicate it to them. But especially we dedicate it to the memory of Louise Robbins, mother of Peter, Andrea, Sheila, and Lindsay, because we both loved her deeply, and wish she were here to see this book . . . .

61390

We wish to thank *Woman's Home Companion, Parents' Magazine,* and *Today's Woman* for their co-operation in permitting us to use some of the photographs that have previously appeared in their magazines.

Library of Congress Catalog Card Number 54-10764

Copyright 1950, 1952, 1953, 1954, by Anna W. M. Wolf and Suzanne Szasz
Copyright, 1953, 1954, by Suzanne Szasz
All Rights Reserved
Printed in the United States
Designed by Alma Reese Cardi

CONTENTS

INTRODUCTION

It is fashionable now, as I suppose it has always been, to pooh-pooh the experts on child care, especially when they write books. Today we are in the midst of a "give the baby back to the mother" campaign, as well as in a period when parents are told to throw the books out of the window and rely on their own common sense. "Eggheads," experts, and books are placed in the same bracket of black-listed subversives. Some experts who before may have gone too far in insisting that parents must follow books closely and specifically are now the most vocal in recommending a feel-your-own-way approach.

But let's give the experts and books their due. They have brought about changes that make it possible for parents to rely on common sense, and to do it safely as well as with conviction and assurance. Take, for example, the matter of preparing a child for hospitalization. Psychiatrists and psychologists, along with some pediatricians, have shown that separation of an infant from his mother may interfere with the child's emotional development, and that hospital care which is hygienic from the medical point of view may be unhealthy from the psychological. Many parents had suspected this all along, but could not get hospitals to change their ways of caring for patients until they had support from the experts. As a result, we now have a small beginning in the humanizing of hospitals, and parents can be given guidance on how to prepare a child for operation (as is done in this book) and can put it into practice with confidence.

I am old-fashioned enough to believe that parents need books as well as other guides to help in child rearing. But these need to satisfy certain standards—high standards. This book meets the test. Here parents will find information which is accurate, and guidance which is practical and time-tested. This book is reassuring. It will help a parent to be himself, natural and not frightened nor unsure. It is interesting. And although its pictures are beautiful portraits, they carry lessons for the person who learns easiest by seeing.

Mrs. Wolf, a long-time member of the staff of the Child Study Association of America, has had many years' experience in counseling of parents, both individually and in groups. She is the author of books and numerous articles on child development and parent-child relationships. Miss Szasz is one of the country's leading photographers and is a perceptive photographer of childhood. Her work appears constantly in national magazines and this is the first time her work appears in a book of her own. They have chosen life-situations which, though common to parents and children in everyday living together, are very significant because around each there often is investment of feeling and emotion. Such charged situations easily become strained; they create problems. There are no cookbook recipes on how to solve problems in this book, but behavior is presented so that with its meaning better understood a parent may deal constructively with his child as an individual.

The tone of the author's guidance is never stern or scolding; neither is it sentimental. It has assurance, as all good teaching should have, yet it is flexible and willing to see all sides. It does not pit one person against another or parent against child. One finds here sensitivity and respect for human beings.

Books such as this are best read in installments. When in doubt, as all parents are from time to time, reference to appropriate chapters will provide ready assistance in dealing with the behavior in question. Of course there is no reason why one should not read it from beginning to end in a single evening. This is what my daughter did after curiosity prompted her to first read the chapter on baby-sitting. From then on there was no way of stopping her. Asked for her opinion about the book, she said in five words what I have been trying to say, "It's neat. It makes sense."

MILTON J. E. SENN, M.D.
Director, Yale University Child Study Center

FOREWORD

No one needs to tell you who are parents that when children are very little they need you almost constantly. Even when they begin to move toward independence, they still turn to Mother a dozen times a day with demands big and little. They expect you to set right whatever in their lives goes even slightly wrong; they want you there to share their discoveries and their pleasures. But you may not know ahead of time that, besides these almost hourly needs, there are certain important moments in a child's life that are harder for him than others and times when he may need your special help and understanding to enable him to go forward and take the next step in healthy, happy development.

This book is an attempt to focus on some of these moments and to make clear to you both visually and in words what may be going on inside your children and how you can best be of help. Suzanne Szasz is no mere illustrator. Step by step throughout this book we have exchanged ideas, planned and worked together. It is her special gift that she is able actually to photograph children's *feelings* and show you in a series of pictures the drama going on within them.

In my experience I have found that parents are better off if they can occasionally share their real doubts with another instead of bottling them up inside. Seeing your own child in the grip of jealousy, you may have secretly wondered, "Is it only my child who has these ugly feelings?" When he bullies another child (or is bullied), when he dawdles over everything or refuses the most reasonable requests, when you see him afraid or a sissy, you may have had moments of anguished doubts. You ask yourself, "Is this the kind of a person my child is going to be?"

It is my hope that this book will make it clear that you are not alone and that these rough moments in your children's development are the stumbling blocks characteristic of early childhood growth; all parents, if they are honest and have eyes to see, will observe one or another of them in some form. I hope too that it will give you a clearer idea of your own important role and help you find ways to make the rough moments smoother. Even more, I would like to believe that as you look and read, the charm of childhood, the joy and challenge of parenthood may become ever more apparent.

There are no rule-of-thumb procedures. In none of these pictures will you find portrayed any "right technique" for meeting a crisis. It is my deepest conviction that, in fact, there are no right techniques. Each of you must find your own special way—the way which feels most comfortable for you and which you find is most helpful for your particular child. But though finally you must learn to trust yourselves, the experiences of others may help deepen your insight, suggest new attitudes, and quicken feelings that somehow serve to smooth the way. These in the end are what will really count.

ANNA W. M. WOLF

HELPING YOUR CHILD'S EMOTIONAL GROWTH

Don't expect
to be perfect

With a baby on the way, prospective parents can't help dreaming a bit. Often their dreams are projected far into the future and are based on the rashest assumptions of what their child will be like. They may think of him as a boy—one perhaps with strong scientific interests (which they of course will understand and foster). Or the baby is to be a girl who will share their tastes and prejudices—a wonderful companion for life. This dream child is a very important person and perhaps does actually help parents get ready for what's ahead, easing the transition to the real child who in all probability will be entirely different. Someday of course they will have to give up the dreams and get acquainted with the actual children that fate sends. For only when they have learned to know each one of their children as individuals will parents be in a position to help them grow up to be the best of what they are.

This may seem obvious, but in practice it isn't so easy. It's always hard to accept any limitations in the people you care for most. And besides—unlike your husband and your friends, you haven't chosen your children; you have had to take what comes—and love them.

But once you have actually met and finally accepted your children, you discover that they are bristling with challenging potentialities. You find too that there are many sources of guidance and information to help you make the most of them. Much can be learned from the experience and study of others. Such a help, I hope, is this book which defines for you some of the more important milestones in a child's development and suggests ways to reach out a helping hand to him. When it comes to books—the best way to read even the best of them is to read and forget. You don't actually forget, of course; you assimilate the knowledge gained and make it so much a part of yourself that you scarcely realize you ever

1

learned it. Another way is to talk things over with an older, much more experienced parent; this can often give you a better perspective. And times may come—and they don't have to be too desperate, either—when professional consultation and advice may be extremely useful.

Another important thing to know is this: being human, you're bound to make some mistakes. The wonderful thing about humans is that they can learn from mistakes and the wonderful thing about babies is that they can survive a good many. Even though you haven't the sure instincts of a mother bird, if you're observant and perceptive and open-minded, you'll eventually acquire certain intuitions and feelings that are a pretty good working basis for knowing how to act in difficult moments.

One of the commonest mistakes of young parents is to try so hard to be perfect and to be so analytical about everything they do that they lose their spontaneity and self-confidence. For example, you may have been made to feel that you must be calm and patient with your children, no matter how unreasonable they are, that it's up to you to give them something called "emotional security" even when your own world is tumbling about your ears. Or you may have hidden within yourself the guilty secret that you find one of your children more attractive and in every way easier to get along with than another, so you lean over back-ward not to play favorites—and this doesn't work either. You begin to doubt that you're really a good mother and so have to keep up a false front even before yourself.

It's not that what you do and feel is unimportant. Patience with children is certainly desirable. So is giving them the feeling that each one is loved and accepted. It *is* bad to play favorites. But parents, like children, have their own unruly feelings, and to tell them to be perfect is a large order—too large. Your children are distinct individuals, and so are you. Though you probably do love one as much as another, you may very well *like* them in varying amounts.

I'd like to propose that parents stop pretending to be perfect and instead settle for doing the best they can. There's no need to feel so guilty about those moments of irritability or of disappointment in one or another of your children; they come to every parent. Don't try so hard that you hide yourself from yourself.

Is there a catch here? If parents honestly face themselves and accept what they find, does this give them a blank check to behave or misbehave, to be as irritable, as angry, as self-indulgent as they please? I think not. If you can be tolerant toward yourself, the chances are you'll be more patient with your child. With your own emotional knots untied, you'll be better able to relax and enjoy your children.

For what I am suggesting isn't license for parents to act as they please. What you say and do must always be subject to thought and control. But parents and children alike will do better when they're free to *feel* as they must. This is actually a first step toward turning those "good" feelings we would like to have into a reality instead of a pretense. With this kind of freedom comes emotional liberation; it is the basis of mental health.

When parents have recognized that they sometimes have hostile feelings toward their children, they can accept with better grace the hostility all children feel at times toward them. A young child indeed often expresses himself with shocking directness.

"I hate you—you're the meanest mother in the whole world," he tells you. Or, about the baby, "I don't care if he is my little brother, I'm going to stuff him down the toilet and flush him into the ocean—yes I am!"

Heavens! How words like that used to terrify and appall you! The thought crosses your mind that you may be just as bad a mother as this child says you are. (Deep within you is the specter of your own "bad thoughts" toward *him*.) And where are your dreams of brotherly love? Have you brought forth a monster?

But as you grow more experienced, this sort of thing won't seem so unnatural. This child of yours is just a human being like yourself, struggling with the same emotions. The only difference is that he hasn't yet learned to hide what he feels. Knowing what you know about yourself, you want above all else to avoid teaching him to hide. He too has the right to feel as he must. Love can then come in its own good time. For there is another truth you have learned: that even if love isn't always in the forefront, it's still somewhere, it can grow stronger, and, for all our ups and downs, it's the cornerstone of our feelings for one another.

"Yes, I know how you feel," you may say. "But lots of the time you do love me a lot—and lots of the time you think John is terribly cute. As you get older those times will come oftener."

Your child breathes easier. My mother doesn't stop loving me even when I'm bad, he thinks, and she says I'll get better.

For a small child this is a great discovery, perhaps the greatest he will ever make. It may very well play the decisive part in his future destinies. It is the basis for emotional security. It is of the very stuff that will make him strong throughout life.

The newborn baby
needs a lot of mother

Is there any one secret to the art of being a successful parent? If I had to commit myself I believe I would answer that in great measure the secret lies in how well you understand the special language of childhood, and those deeper meanings behind simple words and facts. You don't learn this sort of thing in a day. But as young parents get to know themselves and their children, they acquire a kind of sixth sense for this. They come to know instinctively, as we say, what's going on in a child, whether he needs help or whether it's safe to give the colt his head.

Most mothers learn to accept their baby's dependence in the first weeks of life. They really want to answer his summons quickly and yearn to make him comfortable. This isn't always easy. Babies are puzzling little creatures and even healthy ones may have unaccountable pains and discomforts. Every young mother knows how exhausting it is to try to quiet a wailing infant who can't say what's the matter or what it is he wants. But she tries, and the trying itself helps. The baby builds faith that someone is always near when he's uncomfortable. Food and warmth are his obvious basic needs. During feedings he will need time for "burping." But, more than this, babies need to be cuddled, stroked, moved about. They need someone around who smiles at them, talks to them, plays with them, and enjoys them. Deprived of this communion with other loving people, babies don't grow as fast, aren't as alert mentally, and even—so doctors tell us—seem unable to fight infections and serious illness. This doesn't mean that they should be fussed over and handled continually; they need hours of just being let alone, too. For even the most sociable baby, too much is too much, and mothers learn to sense when this moment arrives.

The mother who responds quickly to her own child's needs will get along better than the one who is bound by rules. The only rule that is sure to work is: Don't be bound by rules. For example, when a young baby cries, the mother's impulse is to go and comfort him—and she is right, for crying is an SOS. The small infant can't say what troubles him —he may just need the reassurance of a hand that turns him over or gently pats him back to sleep. Or his discomfort is relieved when Mother holds him upright over her shoulder, pressing one hand against the soles of his feet. He responds sometimes to gentle rocking by growing drowsy and falling asleep. Babies whose crying is respected in this way during the early months of life usually settle down to greater serenity than those whose earliest inarticulate calls for help have gone unanswered, perhaps because of some misunderstood "rule."

Of course, one of the commonest causes for crying is simple hunger. No one knows as well as the baby himself when he needs food, and his demands may bear no relation to the clock or to any arbitrary feeding schedule. Response to these demands is important to a baby's well-being, whether he is being nursed or is a bottle baby.

The mother who wants to nurse her baby should keep him near her during the earliest days, encouraging him to nuzzle and root around her nipple even before she has much milk. From the fourth to the sixth day the milk is likely to come in with a rush and the baby whose appetite isn't dulled by recent bottle feedings attacks his meals eagerly. During these days he may want to be at the breast almost constantly, and it is this hungry tugging that stimulates the milk to flow.

With patience in getting through these early days, most mothers will find that they can nurse their babies. If necessary, supplementary bottle feedings can be given—but after the nursing, never before. When a mother prefers not to nurse and would rather give a bottle, the feeding can still do much to weld a bond between mother and baby. Her enjoyment in holding him in her arms, in giving him the bottle when he's hungry, and her pleasure in him as he takes it are subtly communicated to the baby himself.

As the baby grows he can begin to endure some minor discomforts and delays, can wait a bit for what he wants. Mothers learn too that crying doesn't always mean hunger. Before long the infant who demanded food at all hours of the day and night is willing to fit his needs to a more practicable schedule. So too with other demands. By the time he is three or four months old he may be let alone for a short time to cry, may even forget his wants and go off to sleep. This gradual adjustment to more regular living should be encouraged, yet not forced. If a mother is afraid ever to experiment with a child's capacity to adjust to her needs and to a sensible living routine, she may miss the best moment for getting life on an even keel. She may also deprive her child of a real chance to take a new step forward.

In ways like these, with his parents' help, the infant grows stronger, begins to turn into the child who is learning to live with others in a demanding world. There is no final word or sure rule to help you help him. Even the "demand schedule," followed too literally or too long, becomes as rigid as the old clock-bound schedule. Each baby is as much an individual as his parents, and he deserves to be known and understood and treated as one. There are landmarks along the way, obstacles that can be avoided. Through books, through study, and above all through their own good sense and sensitiveness parents learn to recognize the signs when they appear and acquire the knowledge for dealing with the more common problems when they arise. When this knowledge goes hand in hand with natural good sense, parents will have that self-confidence which best equips them to get their child off to a good start.

ELLEN'S FIRST
THREE MONTHS

After the long months of waiting here's Ellen at last—real, tangible —all seven pounds of her, a complete little girl with tiny perfect finger-nails, delicate brows and lashes. Millions of times the miracle has hap-pened; yet each time the new human being is unique. Never since the world began have any two been just alike.

But it's a good idea for new mothers to know in advance that maternal feeling doesn't always come all at once with a great over-whelming surge. For many, actually, there's a certain letdown feeling after the glow of the first few days. Sometimes the baby's looks are a bit disappointing; he seems to take after someone in the family you don't like very much. His ears may stick out, or his eyes "roll around"; he may have some slight blemish. You wanted a boy and here's a girl—or vice versa. Or you may feel that somehow your husband's enthusiasm lacks conviction. Nursing at first is sometimes tiring and uncomfortable. More often, perhaps, your sense of letdown is vague. You can't explain it and only half admit it to yourself.

These days, these misgivings usually pass quickly. Here's a new human being, your very own, dependent on his parents for every need, utterly trusting. As you care for him your spirits rise, life takes on deeper meanings, and with the first real smile of response you surrender com-pletely to this new enchantment.

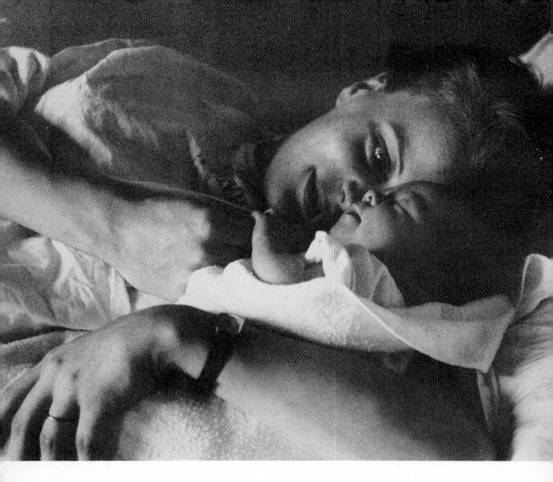

Hospital days are so full of activity that the times just to lie quiet and get acquainted are especially precious. For Ellen's mother, it's a help to have a chance to know and handle her baby before going home. More and more hospitals are providing "rooming-in" arrangements for those who want it. This is a great advantage, especially if you want to nurse your baby. Though scientific evidence favors breast feeding, doctors agree that bottle babies can be healthy, too, and that both babies and mothers are better off when the mother follows her preference.

Home—and a million things to do. But two new parents can always take time out just to gaze and to chuckle.

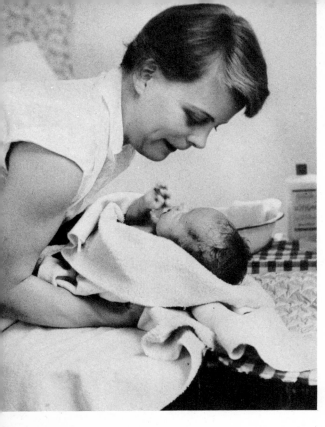

Ellen seems to tiny and fragile. On the first day nothing's quite organized. Safety pins are stubborn. First Mother

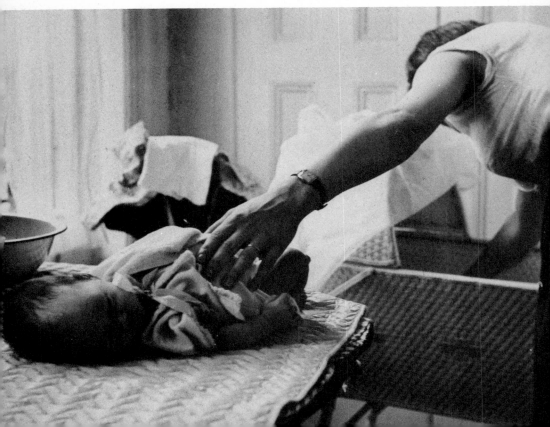

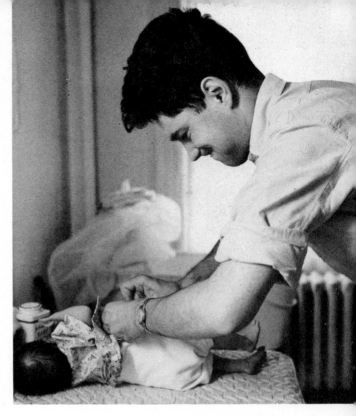

—then Father tries a hand

13   *—and always there are
              diapers to fold.*

When she's either a month old or weighs ten pounds Ellen may go out. Now there are warm sunny hours together in the park.

And moments, too, when for husband and wife feelings run too deep for any words.

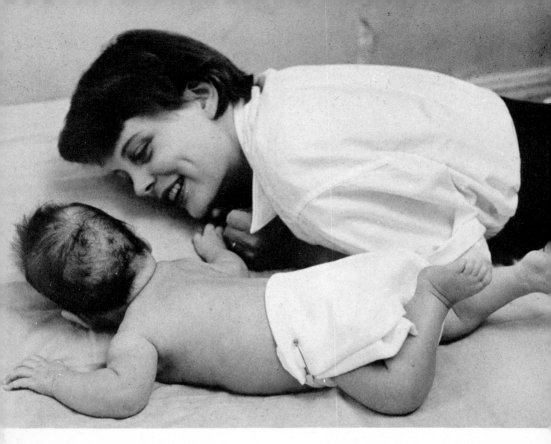

Mother loves those foolish times when she and Ellen just play and talk together. Bath time—one of the high spots of the day—is a lot of fun for both. When she's about six weeks old Ellen really smiles for the first time—a tremendous event.

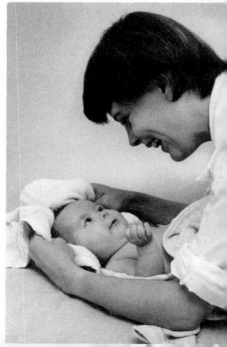

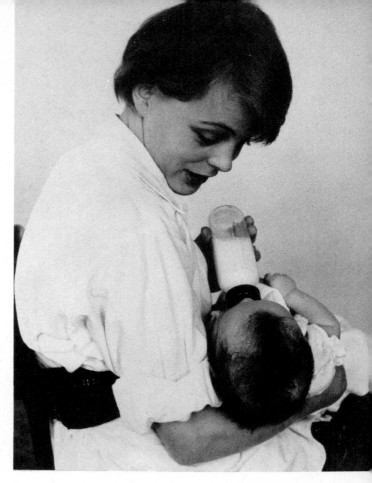

Exhausting times are bound to come when nothing goes right. Meals don't sit well, Ellen takes forever to burp, just wants to be held and rocked all the time.

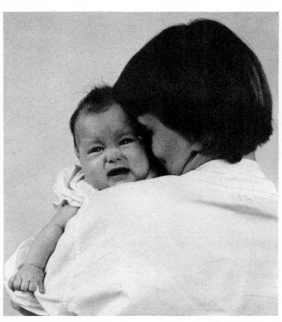

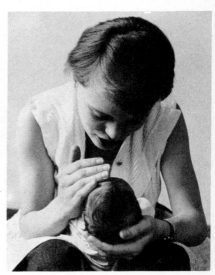

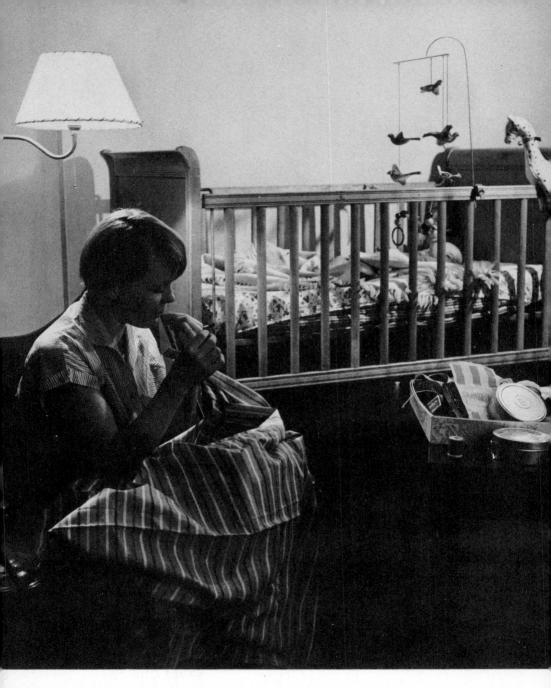

Life isn't all Baby. Chores must still be done. Though a diaper service is a great boon in a home when there's no automatic washer, there are always plenty of extras with a baby in the house. Clean diapers must be folded and stacked. Marketing and cooking must go on as usual, and everything takes longer because Ellen will wake and call for attention.

There's a husband to love and plan for as always. Friends are important, too, and so is dressing up and going out now and then. Young babies are easier than older ones to take to someone's home, don't care where they sleep. Here Ellen, for the moment, is very much awake and obviously the life of the party.

In the dark early morning hours comes the call for food. Mother bounds out of bed from a deep sleep, finds Ellen her most bright-eyed and enchanting self. Only gradually does a baby learn to know night from day and that night is for sleeping. Then once again Mother will get those hours of unbroken rest she had all but forgotten.

Babies may get anxious

When your baby is somewhere between six and ten months old, he may surprise you by suddenly turning shy. Even children who, during their early months, were perfectly composed or almost chummy with outsiders, may begin at this age to be troubled at the appearance of a strange face. By now they have begun to notice facial details, they've learned to expect Mother's face. When a strange one appears instead, you may see a baby's tentative smile change to a stare of surprise and distrust. With some, the corners of the mouth begin to quiver and turn down, the brows wrinkle, and presently the child bursts into disconsolate wails. With others, you may notice nothing more than a sober lack of responsiveness in place of the old outgoing exuberance. With a few babies the reaction seems hardly to exist at all. Psychologists have called this reaction "eight-months anxiety." It is not a cause for alarm; it merely shows that the child can now distinguish the familiar face from the strange one and has a positive preference for the one he knows, usually Mother's. When someone he doesn't expect appears in her place, it troubles him, and he registers his disquiet often vociferously, sometimes more quietly.

If your baby passes through this phase and turns suddenly unfriendly, you may find that some visitors will be downright offended. Others may try to force their attentions on the unwilling victim, thus adding to the child's misery and making it harder for him to feel friendly toward new people as they come along.

To win your baby's confidence, your visitor's best chance is to be sure first that you are close by to give your baby a feeling of reassurance. After this, your friend should stay at a comfortable distance and not pay much attention. She may even turn away to chat casually with you. After a while, if the stranger starts playing with a bright object or new toy, most babies will gradually make cautious overtures. Of course, if the child's discomfort continues, it's best to give up, leave the room, and try again another day. There should be no begging for kisses or attempts at fondling a child who draws away.

This early shyness with outsiders is the result of the young child's fast-developing attachment to the person who usually cares for him—

a bond which will be a close one all through the early years. Although there will be times when it may be inconvenient for parents, the child's healthy mental and emotional growth demands this attachment, and in most families both child and parents find it deeply satisfying.

To a child going through an anxiety period, the withdrawal of the loved face is very disconcerting. If now he suddenly finds himself alone with strangers, he may have to struggle with a real sense of loss. No one can quite convince him that his parents, whom he has learned to trust, will surely return. This is why a child who has been left to the care of strangers may actually turn away from his mother when she does return, as though he has lost faith in her. He may show a new kind of irritability. Little games he once played may now be forgotten, established habits about going to bed or eating may be unsettled again. He may lose his gaiety and responsiveness, almost as though he never again would dare trust himself with strong feeling.

All parents need to get away from their children now and then, but such absences can be planned for times when it is as little disturbing as possible to the child. This means that parents should learn to recognize when he is going through these periods of anxiety, for they aren't limited to "eight-months anxiety," but may appear from time to time during the early years. It may be well to put off absences, if one can, until the child has regained his friendliness and confidence in outsiders. This isn't always possible. Emergencies sometimes come along when parents have no choice but to leave and make the best arrangements they can for a child. Sometimes they can take him along, sometimes they can't.

For the child left at home, the choice of the person who cares for him is very important. This is one of the reasons why every family needs a friend, a relative, a trusted helper whom the child has learned to know and accept. Even if she is not quite as good as Mother, at least the baby has known her for some time, accepts her as someone on whom he can depend and with whom he feels secure and happy. For the baby, Mother's face means "all's well." It means food and warmth, smiles and play, relief from discomforts of all kinds. Only with this blessing upon him can he feel safe. This deep attachment first to the mother, then to one or two other familiar people is the child's foundation for loving others later on. Through them he learns to have confidence in himself and in the world. He is free to go forward and learn.

SUDDENLY,
JOHNNY GETS SHY

Everyone loves a friendly child, the kind who responds with a ready smile when you speak to him, who talks freely and acts naturally. Children vary enormously. Some can plunge right into the middle of things at once. Most, perhaps, are just a trifle shy to start with and some, as we know, are painfully shy. Much may depend on what grownups do at those special periods—the first comes somewhere between six and nine months—when many a child shows signs of discomfort with strangers. This eight-month-old baby had a mother who knew how to help her child at one of those moments that may appear unimportant, yet are often critical.

But something's wrong—it isn't the face he knows. The stranger smiles, but Johnny wants no substitutes.

Johnny is all agog when he hears the door open and looks up, expecting to see Mother.

2

The stranger comes closer while he whimpers, sucks his fingers, and, with his eyes, begs her to change.

He still hopes the strange face will turn into Mother's, but it doesn't, and gradually he begins to feel afraid.

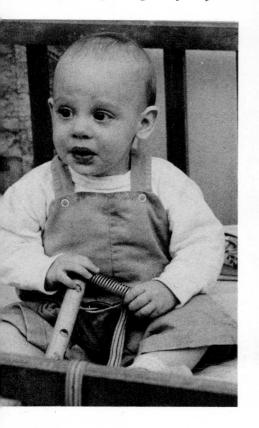

Johnny hasn't seen his mother's friend Elizabeth since he was a friendly baby of four months and received her gladly.

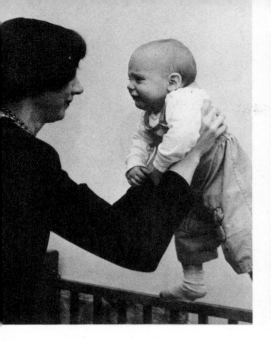
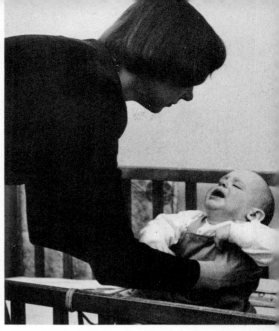

But now he stiffens and begins to cry, showing distress with every tense muscle of his firm little body. Wisely accepting defeat, Elizabeth puts him back, calls to his mother to say that Johnny has forgotten her, and goes about her own business at a distance from the crib. After a minute or so curiosity gets the better of Johnny and he risks peeking.

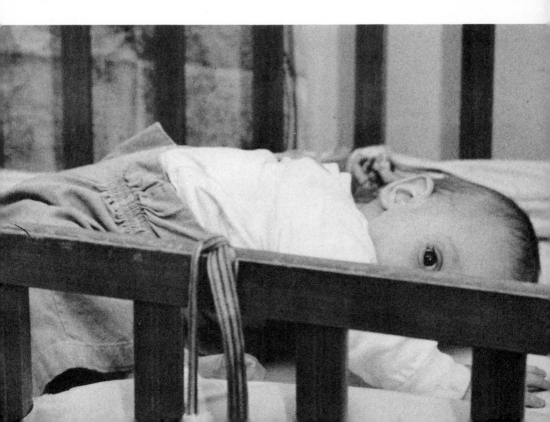

"Just turn your back and ignore him," Mother explains when she returns. "You'll see he'll be friendly again when he's good and ready." She and Elizabeth chat with their backs turned to the baby.

Presently Elizabeth feels a small hand on her shoulder. The hand tugs at her necklace and Elizabeth turns. But it's too soon. Johnny can't take it quite yet and starts bawling again.

Mother picks him up and his troubles are over for the moment. From the haven of Mother's lap the world is quite safe again. Elizabeth isn't so bad after all.

3

By now Johnny is full of giggles, alternately hides his face in Mother's neck, then grabs Elizabeth's nose. Nobody tries to hurry Johnny, and that's the secret of success. Finally Johnny relaxes and is friends at last with the terrible stranger.

The world grows wider

The first world we know is Mother's face. Even when the outside world begins to get its share of attention from a small child, the only way he can fully assimilate and enjoy new experiences is by having an unshakable feeling that Father and Mother are right there where you think they are when you need them. Fortunately, a child usually spends the first year of life in close companionship with the people who are going to be a permanent part of his world. These continuous relationships afford the secure base that will make it easier for him to go out into the wider world of grownups. By planning, ways can be found to assure him of this early companionship without complicating Mother's life too much. A movable crib or basket may come in handy if she wants to keep him near her while she works. When he begins to creep about, a kitchen shelf can just as easily hold toilet articles and a change of diapers as the bath or bedroom, and kitchen cupboards yield a wealth of playthings.

This doesn't mean that a baby should never be left alone. He can be, of course, and may gain too from having to depend on his own resources now and then, and learning that he is safe even when his mother's out of sight. Mothers have to feel their way toward what he can take and what's most comfortable for all concerned. Parents who want to go visiting in the evening will often find it quite practicable to take the baby along and let him sleep at their friends' home till they are ready to leave. An infant does not usually find this break in routine disturbing, and even for older children this may be better than leaving them alone with a stranger.

Started off this way, a child is prepared to venture forth in his own time and with a sound basis on which to build independence and self-reliance. Assured that Mother is near, he can go happily about his own

DOMINICAN COLLEGE
LIBRARY
SAN RAFAEL

affairs exploring all over the house. He stops to grasp and handle everything in reach. He wants to climb stairs and clamber onto chairs and tables. Unaware of danger, he will turn on faucets and gas cocks, lean out windows, sample the contents of shelves and cupboards. Sooner or later he pats the hot radiator—and cries. Or the chair topples over and spills him to the floor. For Mother, the problem is to keep him safe from serious injury without discouraging all this fine zeal for discovery. Although he needs constant watching, the "no-no" formula isn't enough. He also needs to feel that his mother encourages adventures when they are safe and finds ways to make them safe whenever she can.

Very early in life, a child discovers that parents are there to keep little people safe and help them be good. One of the best ways to keep them safe is to put dangerous things away—medicine, disinfectants, matches should be completely out of reach of young marauders; so should household treasures. Windows may need bars; stairs, gates. Homes where young children live can't be just like homes for grownups.

But as children get older, they can learn what they may and may not handle. They can know it's *"never"* for the electric outlet or the flame on the kitchen range; that there are other objects they may handle *"sometimes"* if grownups are around to make them safe. These instructions, if given clearly and simply and in a friendly but serious tone, rarely fail to impress a child who has learned by now that parents mean what they say. Later, the three- to five-year-old can be shown how to strike a match safely and only when a grownup is there to watch, how to climb on a chair without tipping it, how to carry a tray without spilling. There will be mistakes, of course, and parents must be watchful and quick to go to the rescue when needed. But reasonable protection should never become overprotection. When parents must stop a child from doing what's dangerous, the best plan is either to show him how to do the same thing safely or to offer him something else to do that's safe.

Though most children find a lot to do for themselves, there are times when parents need to take the initiative. They can greatly enrich a child's life by providing what's best in picture books and stories, by showing him how to use crayons, clay, and paints, encouraging record playing or other music, getting him to join in family singing and dancing. They can see that children have the chance to run and climb, to get into water and sand, to know animals, to know other children, other grownups. The thrill that comes with learning to skate or ride a bicycle is greater when parents share the thrill.

All this takes time and energy. It asks you to have the kind of flexibility that makes it possible for you to drop what you're doing and really look and marvel at a child's latest discovery. "Look, Mommie, what *I* found!" exclaims a five-year-old, opening his hand to exhibit a dead beetle. Mothers can't afford to be household perfectionists. At any moment they may have to abandon the cleaning or ironing and decide that their children come first. Fathers may have to postpone the job on the car today because a toy needs mending.

But above all it asks you to have on hand at all times enormous funds of patience and selflessness. No wonder you're sometimes weary. It isn't easy to go on day after day giving to a child who makes ceaseless demands yet never cares if you are tired, or notices when you're low-spirited; who never shows gratitude; who can't really speak your language.

There are no sure rules to guide you, either. It's the spirit of give-and-take in the family climate that counts. Yet children eventually do learn, do discover that there is work to do and that there are others in the world beside themselves. Even a young child boiling with excitement can in time learn to wait for his parents' attention. Older ones gradually learn to see you as a person with problems of your own. They learn best and most surely if they're accustomed from the beginning to find parents interested in their lives and in sharing this day-to-day living. On this sure foundation they gain the strength which makes trials and disappointments bearable when they come.

FIRST
ADVENTURES

Meet another Johnny, just a year old. He can't quite walk alone yet, but that doesn't stop him from roving all over and getting into everything. This is how he learns about the immediate world around him—in this case a small apartment high up above the street in a great city. His mother lets him rove the premises, knowing that this is how he'll develop both muscles and mind. Wisely she puts what breakables she can out of his reach, but she knows she has to be alert and watch for the unpredictable. Mother is gradually teaching him what "No, no" means. Quietly she sits beside him, extends his hand toward a forbidden object, then pulls it back, saying "No," and shakes her head. The look on her face is serious. But she knows it takes time for babies to learn self-control and that for many months while the teaching goes on she'll have to take time to keep him out of trouble while she encourages whatever adventures are safe.

Johnny can now play alone for short times, especially if someone takes the trouble to get him started. Every once in a while, of course, he comes back to Mother for attention, and she will have to start him going again. Like most babies, he'll be constantly underfoot interrupting any orderly, efficient routine. It's tiring, of course, with a lot of leg and back work, and takes quick thinking, but Mother knows there is little that is more important than helping a baby discover the world.

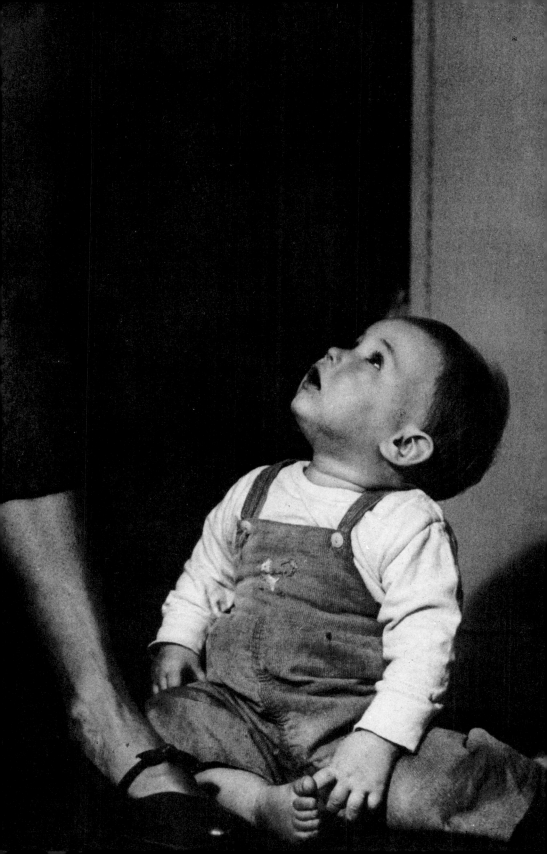

Here's something definitely not for small fingers. But for Johnny, what a temptation! For a year-old child who watches everything grownups do, what's more fun than taking an object out of a box and putting it back again, or pulling metal prongs in and out of slots? He can't know that this may really be dangerous and there's no way to teach him "by experience." Mother has two jobs: first to anticipate and prevent moments like this by watchfulness and by keeping Johnny busy elsewhere, and second to teach him the meaning of "No."

Small children learn gradually, and it will be a long time before a mother can depend on prompt obedience from a small child. Hand slapping and punishments are no more effective than quick action and a firm serious "No" spoken in a voice that a child knows means business.

Johnny hears Mother shout and from the tone of her voice senses a moment of danger. He pulls his hand away, startled. The look on her face says as plain as her words, "No, no, Johnny, you must never touch that."

Turning the light switch on and off proves to be just as much fun, and Johnny does it over and over again.

He gets into everything. First the record player. He can heave the big books off their shelves, too. And the food closet's the best of all.

But he happily settles for a kettle and lid to play with when Mother shows him how. Oh, what a heavenly noise! He bangs away happily.

Next there's a game of peek-a-boo with the curtains. Later the pursuit of his favorite toy brings problems. Shall he try to get Teddy back? Or just flop down on top of him?

Johnny, like most one-year-olds, eats a variety of foods—when he wants to.

He's awkward with a spoon but can learn only by practice. At this age most children need Mother to help guide the spoon to the mouth, but later in the meal, as appetite wanes, she may have to take over the feeding completely.

4

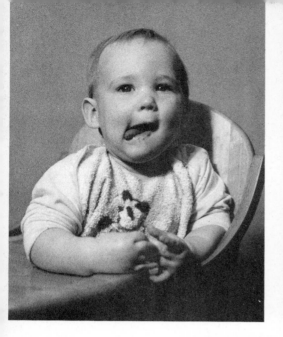

What's for dessert? Hope it's prunes. Or applesauce. Horrors! It's new food with a strange bad taste. Mother takes her cue. No more of that today.

5   *Milk is his old stand-by! But how to take it? Johnny is gradually getting used to a cup, but it takes time.*

Sometimes he just likes to sit on the floor beside Mother and lean against her while they chatter quietly. He loves to listen to Mother sing, too, especially when he can climb onto her lap and put his face on her shoulder. "More, more," he says.

Mother has asked her friends please not to phone her at this hour of the day. Johnny's entitled to some time without interruptions. This quiet hour at the end of his day, when nobody's hurried or rushing around, when a child feels safe and sheltered in his small cozy world, makes it easier for him gradually to quiet down, to separate his thoughts from the exciting doings of the day and accept bed and sleep. Johnny's mother and father plan so they still have evenings for themselves after Johnny's tucked in bed.

From this secure home port Johnny will be all ready again tomorrow to sail out once more in search of new adventures in his ever-expanding world.

MEGGI STEPS OUT

It's a big day for the whole family when your baby first steps out into the world all by himself. No wonder everyone is proud; so much has led up to this great event. When he was a baby you provided him with the right diet for building sound bones and strong muscles. When he was very little you gave him a chance to exercise—kicking and squirming to his heart's content, then to pull himself along on his tummy. Pretty soon you had to keep him safe while he explored the world on all fours. Later, when he got up on his two feet and roved around clinging with his hands to chairs, tables, skirts, and trouser legs, you encouraged him every step of the way and showed your pleasure in each new achievement.

Even healthy babies vary a good deal in the age when they walk alone. Very heavy ones tend to walk later than thin wiry types. Some seem to be cautious and won't risk a tumble. Yet somewhere between eleven and seventeen months the miracle happens, your baby walks. Viewed from his immense new height, his world becomes a new and wonderful place.

The great moment has come for Meggi, aged eleven months, as for the first time she steps away from Mother's steadying hand. Plunk! Down she goes. But the familiar voice and touch give her courage.

She picks herself up and tries again. Walking alone on two feet is terribly exciting, and Mother and Dad are excited too. And there's Daddy, whose outstretched arms are worth reaching.

Only two more steps — and there she is.

The return trip is uneventful. She seems to fly. If she just keeps moving forward, walking isn't a bit hard; it's fun, it's wonderful. It means that a baby has turned into a child with a new place in the world, new dignity. At such a moment it's hard to know who's proudest —Meggi or her parents.

Toilet training may not be simple

Time was when people thought that the sooner toilet training began the better. It was even a matter of rivalry among mothers, a matter of pride to parents if their child was trained early. But today we understand how closely toilet training is bound up with a child's later feelings about his body and all its functions. We have learned to value healthy emotional development above early cleanliness.

We realize now that there is no magic moment when toilet training should begin. The time to start is when the child himself seems ready. An observant mother can usually guess when her baby is likely to go along with her wishes and feel pride and pleasure in acquiring this new skill. Though children differ, training for bowel control may usually be started between twelve and eighteen months of age, not earlier. It is about this time that the bowel movements begin to be regular, coming once, twice, or three times a day at fairly predictable hours. Here is your opportunity to take the child to his own toilet chair and show him what you expect. Don't be shocked if he wants to look at and admire what he learns to put there. This is a natural response and it gives you a chance to show how pleased you are too with his new achievement. Later, you can let him help you flush the toilet. The more he can manage to do for himself the better.

With this sort of management, most children get fair bowel control during the first half of their second year, though lapses often occur later than this.

Bladder control usually takes longer. With most children daytime control comes during the latter half of their second year. The time to begin training is when dry periods get longer and wetting comes at more regular intervals. The usual times, of course, are first thing in the morning, before going outdoors, after coming in, after lunch, after naptime, and again before going to bed, varying with each child's habits. Nighttime training is likely to come later. Most children achieve dry beds between two and a half and three years of age or thereabouts, and should certainly have achieved it before five. Sometimes it helps to take a child up late in the evening, but it's hardly worth rousing him from sleep if he resists strenuously. Many learn to sleep right through and keep dry without a nighttime trip to the bathroom. Much depends on getting a child really to want to stay dry and to feel that whatever his parents do is done to help him.

A child will need patient help and encouragement from his parents all along the line, if he is to learn successfully the complex muscular responses needed for control. For parents, diapers are a cumbersome nuisance; so is the wet bed. It isn't easy to be patient. Friends and relatives whose children were trained months earlier take an irritating pleasure in hinting it's all easy enough if you know your job. And a mother's own good nature runs out when a bright healthy child insists on wetting or soiling just after he has been taken from the toilet. How long should they put up with this state of affairs, parents wonder.

Here, if we aren't careful, are the makings of a first-rate tug of war, for the whole subject is complicated by obscure emotions and strong feelings on the part of both parents and children. The two-year-old child, for example, feels quite differently from grownups about body excrements; they do not disgust him. On the contrary, observing how much importance his mother attaches to them, he soon comes to regard them as something fine he has made and has a right to value. When he moves his bowels or urinates at his mother's urging, it is disappointing to see her hastily flush his achievement away or show disgust. He sees no reason why she should jerk his hand away when he wants to handle his stool or when he puts his hand in the toilet bowl.

For their part, parents labor under a great burden of private personal history that colors their attitudes toward their children's toilet training. If they were, as children, taught to attach great weight to "regular habits," some are likely to pass this feeling on to their own children by being rigid, tense, and fussy in their demands. Others, aware perhaps of their own parents' mistakes, react too sharply in the other direction; they let training go so long that unconsciously they almost encourage a child to remain a baby. Still others have just heard a lot about the dangers of "forcing," and so they neglect the necessary teaching. Believing they should let a child "train himself," they fail to give even sympathetic help. All these extremes fail to meet the real needs of the child who, as he gets older, grows increasingly aware that most children his age have learned control. Why hasn't he been able to? he wonders. And why doesn't Mother help him?

Even after the age when he can control himself if he wants to, a child who is angry at grownups or engaged in a battle of wills with his mother may balk. With this new-found power he can punish her by refusing to comply with her wishes. This deadlock is less likely to develop if parents keep relations with their children as free from strain and unnecessary conflict as they can.

At the time that toilet training is going on, the child is learning much else besides. How his parents act about this matter, the very expressions on their faces may instill attitudes in a child not easily changed in later life. Parents' attitudes are quickly felt and deeply registered. If they show only disgust at a child's normal interest in his body products, he is all too likely to feel that everything connected with the body is "bad" and should be put out of mind as soon as possible. This is likely to be a handicap to wholesome sex functioning in later life. What's needed is some lighthearted acceptance of the body and its workings and teaching that is timed to take best advantage of the child's own eagerness to grow up.

VICKI
LEARNS

Vicki's mother is one of a good many modern parents who knows the pitfalls of the strict, rigid form of toilet training administered when a child is too young. In her eagerness not to force matters she tended to go too far in the other direction. She didn't give Vicki the steady, consistent help children need. Like many mothers today, she was uncertain of what to expect. This made Vicki, too, uncertain of her own powers of control.

But now that Vicki is two and a half, Mother realizes that she was so unsure that she may have missed some important moments when she might have helped. There seems no doubt either that Vicki herself will be much better pleased with life when she no longer wets herself. Fortunately Mother is equally aware that a sudden crackdown now would be the worst possible course, calculated to produce nothing but bewilderment in a small child. Certainly help is needed for Vicki if she is to go ahead and achieve, in a wholesome way, this important step in development. Real help must be given in an atmosphere that is gentle, encouraging, and friendly. It's clear to Mother that in spite of her own leniency and Vicki's refusal to learn, the child would be more pleased with herself if, like most children her age, she could keep dry.

Mother explains to Vicki quietly and seriously that she is quite able now to use the toilet like grownups. Mother will help by taking her to the bathroom now and then, and Vicki will try to use it. She doesn't rush Vicki, but encourages her as far as possible to manage her own toilet seat and climb onto it. A floor potty chair might have been better for the purpose.

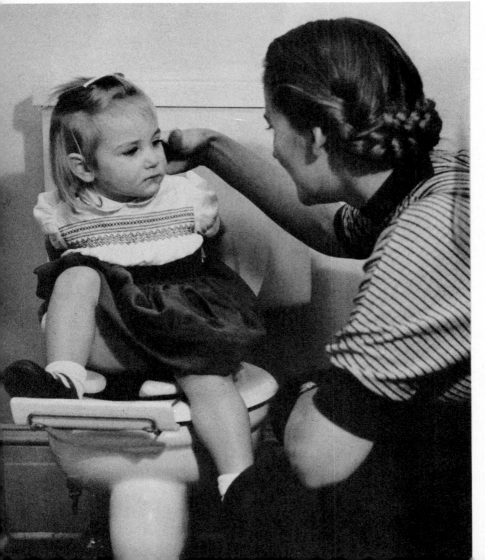

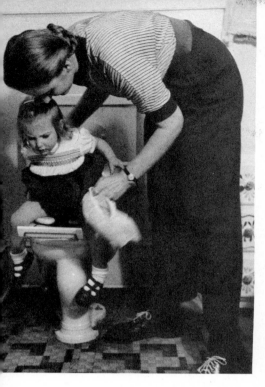

In a little while Mother helps Vicki climb down again. "Oh well, better luck next time," she says hopefully. "Next time——" repeats Vicki, still a bit doubtful. Like most children of her age, she's fascinated by the toilet and might like to handle its contents. Mother discourages this but lets her look in and flush it to her heart's content.

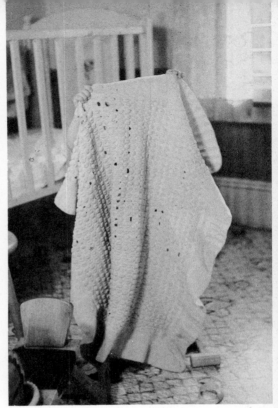

One look at Vicki's face after her nap tells Mother that she has wet her crib again. Vicki tries to be defiant about it but is really unhappy and ashamed. At such moments children often turn to thumb-sucking, to a beloved doll or toy animal or whatever seems to promise consolation. For Vicki it's an old battered blanket that she's clung to since she was a baby. Now it serves the additional purpose of something to hide behind.

With the blanket held close, Vicki's ready to defy the whole world. Almost but not quite. Furtively she watches Mother putting dry things on her bed, finally crawls under a table. Though Vicki has never said a word, Mother knows she's feeling bad and will go to her presently with a friendly word and suggestion that they play something together.

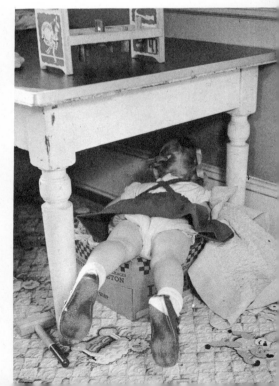

But with Mother's reminders and regular help in actually getting to the bathroom and onto the toilet seat, Vicki gradually learns she can wait, can keep herself dry most of the time. The day comes when she takes the initiative. Now Vicki tells Mother when she has to go. She's ready to wash her hands afterward, too, just as grownups do, and even learns to blow her own nose.

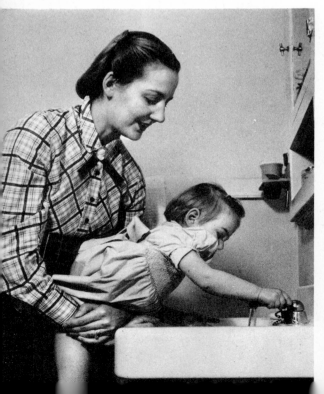

Toilet time's no longer the unhappy time it used to be. Vicki can see by Mother's face how pleased she is, and she herself is mighty happy to be so grown up. With many children, one new step forward brings general all-round maturing. Vicki even looks older, begins to find all kinds of new skills an exciting challenge.

Discipline

Of all the questions that bother parents today, discipline is by all odds highest on the list. We know children need both freedom and discipline. "But how much of each?" we ask, "and at what ages?" It's no easy trick to combine discipline with freedom and initiative, and what parent isn't secretly pleased to see his offspring exhibit a dash of rebellion? We love it! We respect children for their healthy individualism and don't want to crush it, but we know the world can hurt them unless they learn to accept some rules and an occasional firm "No."

I have seen families in the past where discipline seemed to be nothing more than a set of maneuvers to make a child behave in a way that wouldn't interfere with the grownups. More recently I have seen families where "anything goes" and the children run roughshod over both toes and feelings of others. Neither of these extremes is healthy. Nor is good discipline merely a system of rewards and penalties; it has nothing to do either with spanking or deciding never to spank. It is a whole way of life, based on a knowledge of what children need at various stages of growth and of how they're likely to feel about themselves and the people in their world. Success with discipline depends largely on the parents' own good sense, their ability to learn, and their intuitive feeling for what their child is up against at a particular moment.

Even a young child needs some freedom, the right to explore his surroundings and even to make a few not too costly mistakes. But when he is young he must feel that his parents are at the helm and as he grows older he should expect them to throw their weight on the side of his own emerging conscience and find ways to help him go forward. For their part, parents must understand how hard it is for a small child to be good, how long it takes to learn, and how important it is to keep alive, too, a child's impulse to be active, experimental, and questioning.

Even the best of children aren't invariably loving and reasonable. It helps to know that yours aren't the only ones who have moments or even longer periods of hostility and resentment. Most of us start by believing that if we are gentle and patient with a child he will surely respond in kind. In the long run, of course, we are right. But many a conscientious parent can testify that at times children can be blindly hostile, swept by inner storms or by anger that is hard for parents to cope with, even harder to understand. It takes time for them to see these crises with some detachment and to realize that theirs is not a hopelessly difficult child nor they themselves failures as parents.

Such outbursts can't be dealt with either by passive acceptance or angry retaliation. What's needed are some positive measures which will help relieve tensions—improved relations to one or both parents, to a brother or sister, to friends, or a happier time in school. Why, we must ask, is our child discontented and therefore angry at the world? This is a basic question and much depends on how skillful we are at finding answers. But in spite of all appearances to the contrary, at the actual moment of crises children really want their parents to keep them within bounds. In their heart of hearts they don't truly want to be bad. If you make no move to control them, they will feel you have abandoned them to impulses too strong for them to master, and so will be overwhelmed by a sense of guilt and failure. Setting certain clear and simple limits to all the unruly impulses children have, though it is only a part of what's called for, meets an unspoken need in children themselves; without it they feel insecure and troubled.

Most parents live busy lives with small children underfoot in a household where grownups too have needs and where emergencies seem to occur daily. In circumstances like these they would be superhuman if they never nagged, got angry, or slapped. Under pressure they may find themselves punishing impetuously instead of taking time to get at the root of the child's troubles. Or they take the easiest course and succumb to the child's demands, settling for peace at any price. Neither of these extremes helps much; neither is what we mean by discipline.

Think of discipline not as punishment, then, but as the hundred little things a parent can do before punishment is needed. It's the Sunday well planned so children aren't bored or parents irritable. It's the fun with mother in the kitchen and father in the garage. It's the anticipation of those dreadful collisions between Johnny and his grandmother and the ingenuity and effort that go into finding something they might enjoy doing together instead. It's help given quickly at those moments when Mary dawdles over her dressing and when David snatches another's toy—the tact and skill that smooth matters out and restore peace. It's the willingness to stop and think what it is a child *needs,* and decide whether it's the same as what he says he *wants.* It's the parents' resourcefulness in finding ways for children to be active and busy. It's being able to say a firm but friendly "No" to whatever is really out of the question and to say it even when a child uses every known trick to get his way.

Where parents trust their own decisions and children have learned that they mean what they say, it's the rare child who can't eventually accept control. With this matter-of-course authority, punishments are seldom necessary; neither are rewards and bribes. Sure of his parents' pleasure and interest, a child learns gradually to put up with the rough spots and the disappointments. The feeling that his parents are basically for him, not against him, makes all the difference. Home is a place where he can learn and grow, where he is sure he's wanted, knows he belongs.

At the playground there's a very tall ladder that goes right up to the sky. Two-year-old Morgan hasn't a doubt he can make it to the top. All it takes is one step at a time, holding tight to the steps. So he's on his way. Three steps up, Morgan turns around to see a frightening new world far below him and suddenly begins to whimper. He tries still another step. Then Mother comes. "That was fine," she says encouragingly as her hands go round him. "But come back now. Let's see if you know how to climb down too."

WHEN MOTHER SAYS NO

Small children keep parents constantly hopping. How can one keep them safe without frustrating the urge to adventure which is of the very fiber of a healthy child? It takes back work, leg work, and head work to keep up with the incessant urge to explore. Energy runs way ahead of judgment. Seeing her two-year-old in trouble, little Morgan Hall's mother wisely refrains from anxious shouts from afar. She goes to him,

Back on the ground again, and Morgan's big adventure is over. Once more he's only a little boy—and very angry at Mother. But she tells him there's something else to do instead.

steers him into safer channels until his self-confidence and skill are greater.

Good day-to-day management, the knack of spotting trouble ahead before it has actually happened—these, far more than punishments or commands, are the essence of good discipline. This kind of help gives a child the assurance that someone is watching over him who will even save him from himself when necessary. With this approach, most children after a brief storm of protest accept the inevitable and find something else to do.

On the seesaw he can push hard with his feet and go shooting up. Mother laughs because now he can be taller than she is. Morgan laughs too and is happy. Someday he'll be ready to climb the ladder again.

1

FRIENDLY
BUT FIRM

Every mother discovers that no matter how well she manages or how resourceful she is at helping her children find happy solutions to their small daily probems, times come when certain jobs have to be done. The routines of the day must go on. Here's where Mother's own self-assurance and conviction count heavily. Giving orders—and failing to follow through with them—threats, bribery, and nagging at such moments only add to a child's uncertainty about what's expected. The result is discontent and unhappiness for the child as weil as parents.

Sheila's mother has found that prompt action is far easier for everybody than shouting orders, nagging, or even punishment. Sheila herself is learning that somehow hard jobs get done, that she has a mother who can take small tempests in her stride—and restore calm.

Sheila hears Mother say, "Time to clear up now and get ready for supper," and, like every other child her age, gets suddenly absorbed in play and pays no attention. This time it's stringing beads.

The beads all gone, she dumps them off the string again and gets to work with her blocks. Anything to delay the fatal hour! But Mother is coming.

At this moment Sheila's a small bundle of rebellion—shouts defiance, refuses to help Mother clear up. Mother talks quietly, acts quickly.

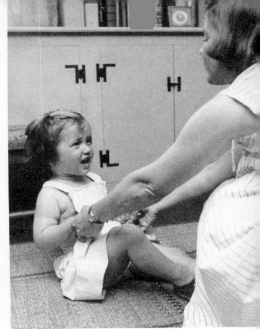

"*I don't like you,*" *says Sheila, covering her eyes and kicking her feet.*

"*Well, well,*" *says Mother,* "*never mind, we'll go get washed and I'm going to tell you a story about three bears and a girl named Goldilocks.*" *She takes Sheila quietly by the hands.* "*Come on now, old thing,*" *she says.* "*There was a mother bear, a father bear, and a baby bear.*"

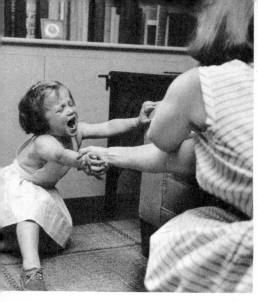

It's no go. Sheila's still furious—pays no attention. So Mother picks her up, tucks her under her arm, and carries her off to the bathroom. All this took exactly three minutes.

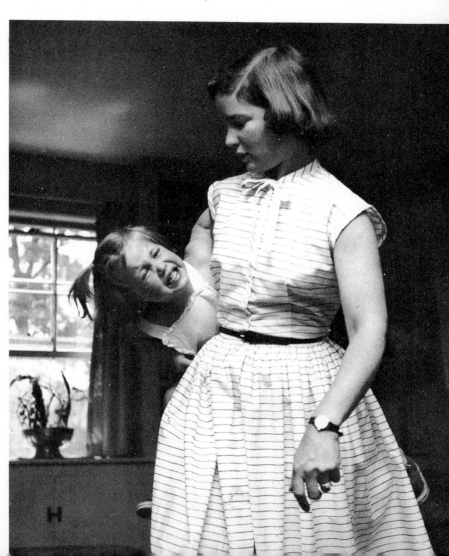

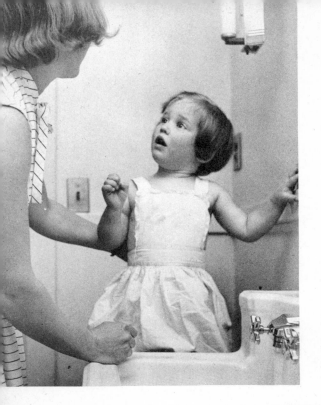

*"What was that girl's name?"
asks Sheila suddenly. "Did she
really have bears? I want a bear."
Mother starts the story, then fills
the basin with warm water.*

*"Was Goldilocks real-
ly asleep in the little
bear's bed? Did she
really jump out the
window? What did her
mommy say when she
got home? Tell me that
story again, Mommy."
Hand washing's no
problem now.*

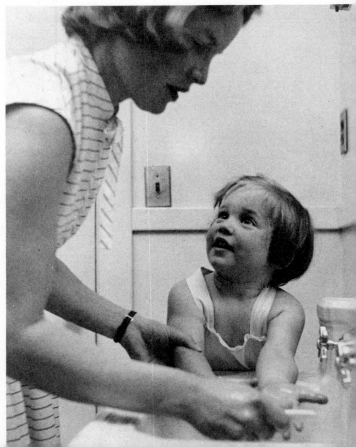

Sheila feels very happy and loving now and will want to hear the story of the Three Bears all over again at suppertime. It's good to have a mother who knows just how to help.

LEARNING
TO SHARE

Sharing possessions with others is no small problem for anybody at any age, and when you're a small child there's a long hard road ahead. Parents and other grownups are most helpful when they can accept wide individual differences in children and when they don't preach or punish or try to force a child to be more unselfish than he can be. But they also need to lead the way, patiently showing how we all must learn to get along with others. Gradually children discover that the best possession of all is friends who like to come to your house and play with you.

There's no formula for success, nor does it ever come all at once. There are some children in whom selfishness and bullying are symptoms of deeper discontent, which must be understood and helped at the source before they can find the strength and security to do anything but demand more and more and cling desperately to everything. But most, when there are resourceful grownups around, do learn—not in one lesson or two or three, but in long continuous exposure to a way of life that includes the rights and happiness of others.

Here's a youngster who seems to have everything in her favor — a happy home, toys, others to play with, parents who love her. Yet more than most children she finds it hard to share, hard to play fair. Mother has learned to expect moments like this — has learned, too, that punishments aren't the answer.

Her friend Billy, the easygoing sort, surrendered the truck and turned to block building. But Susan's still not satisfied, and the moment his back's turned — wham! She demolishes the tower to its foundations.

But here's Mother. *"That was too bad,"* she says, *"but maybe if we all try we can build it up again."* Susan knows that nobody can be pleased with her when she spoils their fun. Mother knows there's more to Susan's problem than can be settled this way alone.

Life can have terrors

A youngster's day is full of novelty in a way that no adult's can be, for almost everything he encounters is new to him. Most of these experiences are pleasant, but now and again a child will meet something quite commonplace and familiar to his parents and find it completely overwhelming. It is these daytime ogres—invisible to the adult eye—that so often haunt a child at bedtime.

The mechanical bunny that seems to us so appealing hopping along the floor is eyed anxiously by a small girl as she edges away. The old man down the street with the funny hat for some reason strikes fear in the breast of our five-year-old son; he hurries past on his way to school and looks the other way.

To grownups a haircut is only a haircut; many youngsters too, can take it as a pleasant adventure. But there are a surprising number to whom the man with the shears may be the embodiment of terror, the devastating fulfillment of some deep dread which parents can't fathom and the child can't explain. It's no use assuring him that the barber is "such a nice man" who "only wants to make us more beautiful"—the child's dread goes beyond anything common sense can reach.

However foolish it all may seem to grownups, such intensity of feeling in a child should be a warning to go slow, and let him come to the new experience in his own way and in his own good time. For Mother, it's an unexpected nuisance when she gets to the beauty parlor just a half hour before lunch, to have her three-year-old daughter first get restless and anxious, then demand to go home, and finally, when lifted into the chair, go into paroxysms of terror and despair. "You might think she was going to her execution!" thinks the exasperated mother. Actually, the child sees it just about like that.

We know that using force with a frightened child increases his terrors and in addition makes him feel that the whole world's against him. Though he may seem to cheer up later and forget all about it, there's always the chance that he doesn't really forget, and childhood terrors have a way of leaving marks. A better plan would be to say good-by and thanks just the same to the barber and go home with the hair uncut. Later perhaps the same child may look on with interest while Mother cuts her big sister's hair. Or she may go quite happily to the beauty parlor and watch while Mother herself undergoes the dreaded operation. Here she has a chance to make friends with the barber, especially if she is fully assured that he won't try to touch her hair. Perhaps he'll let her borrow his shears and have fun snipping the pieces of hair that have fallen to the floor. Or, with him directing, she can cut a tiny snippet from her own locks. At home she might play "beauty parlor" with a doll. Now *she's* the man with the shears and fully in control. The chances are she'll play the part with gusto.

In this way small children learn that what they have feared is really harmless and their anxieties gradually fade. It may take time, and parents need to know that much is at stake. In the end, both for child and Mother, patience and the long way round is the best. When the daytime fears fade, nighttime troubles are likely to be lessened too.

HAIRCUTS FRIGHTEN LESLIE

A child's fears are never "funny"—never something to take lightly. Neither should they be ignored indefinitely; children must know that the time comes when they will have to face up to something hard and learn to cope with it. But rarely is the shortest way the best way. Forcing any terrifying experience on a child usually makes things worse, not better. Time and understanding help most—and the child's knowledge that his parents know how hard it is and want to help.

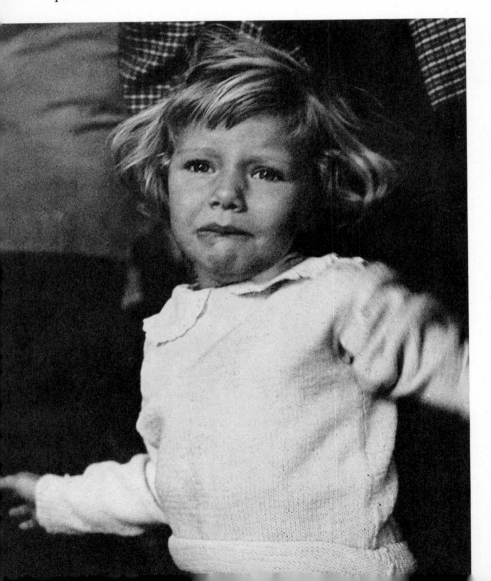

When three-year-old Leslie realizes what's in store for her at the beauty parlor, not even the most beautiful balloon, a present from the barber, can make her forget her fears. Forced into the chair, she's in an agony of terror and misery. Explanations don't help her.

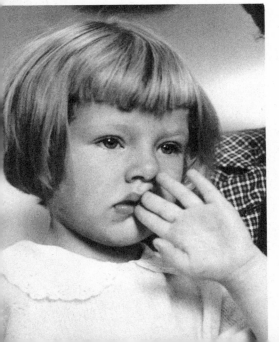

The ordeal over, Leslie is urged to admire the results in a mirror. Neat well-brushed hair is no consolation. Being little seems to mean you're in constant danger from strong grownups who can hold you and make you do whatever they want.

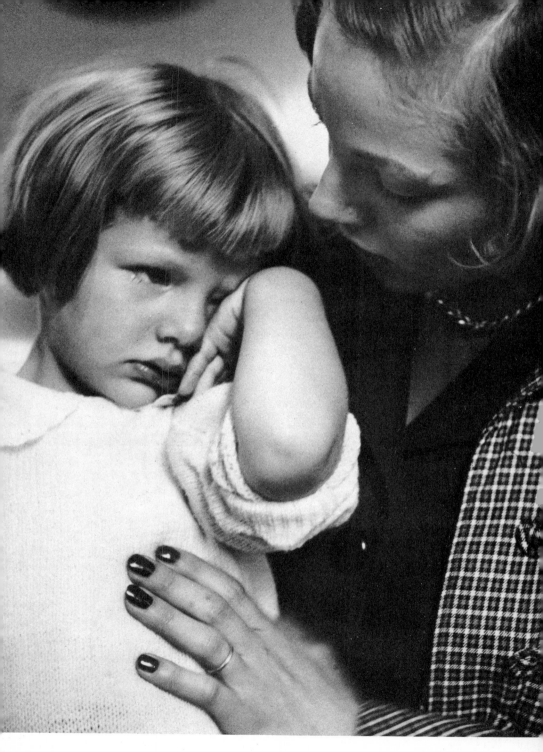

Mother's kindness and consoling words come too late. Leslie's not sure she can ever forgive or trust her again. Later she will appear to forget. But will she?

Bedtime problems

Why do so many children today seem to have trouble going to sleep?

Is it because parents tend to be a bit too easygoing about it? They have been confused, perhaps, by the "permissive" approach, which as applied to eating has worked well; the flexible meal schedule for infants seems to have resulted in fewer food problems than there used to be. A baby will take about what nourishment he needs. But it has not worked for sleep. It's the rare child who knows when he's tired. He *wants* to stay up but he *needs* to go to sleep. A wise mother learns this and finds ways to help him understand that when the time comes, he must go to bed and stay there.

There are other simple measures to help ease this trip to bed and they will save both parents and children much anguish. For one thing, play before bedtime should be kept quiet and unexciting. There should also be a regular bedtime hour which the child knows can only be changed for very special reasons, and for children under six years this should almost never be later than eight o'clock. Parents should make the transition to bedtime gradual. No child should be sent off to bed abruptly. After fair warning has been given that bedtime is at hand, you can go about quietly starting the familiar preparations, creating around this rite a cozy, unhurried, intimate atmosphere. A story, a chat, or a song after a child is tucked in all help quiet a youngster, leaving him with a lingering sense of Father's and Mother's protective presence.

Usually these familiar bedtime rituals, if consistently carried out, will be enough. After one or two brief protests—the last drink of water, the night light perhaps by the bed—most children settle down. If, after this, the two- or three-year-old escapes from his crib, he should be gently but firmly returned and told to stay there. If going to bed has been a a time of fun and affection, neither too hurried nor prolonged beyond all limits of common sense, most children accept the inevitable. Sometimes a child may need his mother's promise to come back and peek at him once more. With this assurance that Mother has not gone for good a child can relax and usually falls asleep before the time for the next promised visit comes round.

But with some children the trouble lies deeper and needs more help. Even when they don't directly say so, children are often uneasy about going to bed. In varying degrees they go through periods when they are afraid—when strange noises, thunderstorms, imaginary animals, or almost anything may seem threatening. They may begin to wonder about death and so about sleep. Or some familiar object, half seen in the subdued light, may assume a dreadful shape. Alone in the dark everything seems strange. Even in the daytime most children worry when Mother dissapears for a while and are afraid she'll never come back again. The loneliness and the dark revive this fear and magnify it. Words and promises that may be accepted during the day fail to carry conviction in the dark.

The eternal charm of "peek-a-boo," we are told, is essentially the child's attempt to assure himself that what is lost can be made to return. "Where's Mother?" you say, covering your face. The baby knits his brow and frowns anxiously, then he snatches the handkerchief away and shouts with glee. He can *make* his mother come back; he can do it again and again. The more you play this with him, the more secure he feels, the more certain that no matter what happens Mother will come back again.

Nighttime fears seem commonest in children around three or four years old. This is the time when they are most dependent on their parents but at the same time are wrestling with many obscure feelings—anger toward Mother or Father, perhaps, with dislike of a brother or sister, or with much else that they know is unacceptable. A child's anxieties are increased by his belief that because of them he somehow deserves punishment. Although he may not put this into words, we have learned that this idea often lurks at the bottom of children's unexplained fears.

Many a sound sleep has been disturbed by wails from the other room or an anguished call for "Mummy!" You're tempted to say, "He's just doing it for attention." Your youngster seems happy the moment you're there; with his familiar world restored all appears to be well. You wonder, "Was it worth getting up for?" Yet this very reassurance may be what he most needs. Left to cry it out, he may only become wider awake and underneath his deliberate bid for attention there may lie anxieties which he himself isn't fully aware of.

The best plan is to try, at the first sign, to keep fears from snowballing up into something unmanageable. This means taking them seriously in these early stages. In the first months and earliest years your prompt and reassuring presence can prevent future trouble. Go and comfort a disconsolate baby. Before leaving any child with someone he doesn't know, make sure that he has already learned to accept the stranger happily. Even when an older child wakes and calls, although he can't say just what's wrong, one of his parents may have to go to his bed and settle him down again with comforting words. Which of us has never waked in the clutches of a nightmare and struggled to throw it off? To a childthese phantoms have even more reality.

If we grant all a child's wishes, will it spoil him? Does the time come when a child should put up with a certain amount of anxiety and perhaps even gain strength by facing his fears alone? These are fair questions.

To answer the first question first: Yes, it is possible to overdo your attention. For instance, no matter how much he begs, it's better not to take a child into bed with you to comfort him. The need will probably grow on him and, in the end, sleeping in his parents' bed creates more troubles than it cures. Short of this, you will find that patience pays off in the end, and gradually your youngster will learn that the night is safe after all and that parents, though out of sight, are still there and haven't forsaken him. As to the second question: There is no general answer to just when children should be expected to face trials alone. Certainly it is possible to go on giving protection past the point where a child is really much frightened and might well be more independent. You might try him out now and then to see if he's strong enough to go it alone.

One way to help a child with nighttime fears is by taking thought for what he may be struggling with by day. Whatever builds a child's all-round self-confidence will help him face the night with less anxiety. He should be encouraged to help himself with daily routines, to learn to climb and run, to play and make things. Within the bounds of safety, he needs to go adventuring beyond nursery walls, to enjoy animals and make friends with children. He can't at first do these things alone, but with your help he can take the first steps.

Perhaps, too, there have been unpleasant experiences during the day that are troubling a child. If there has been anger between you and him, peace should be made before nightfall. Sometimes a child is troubled by a quarrel with a friend. Some seemingly trivial experience may have been a frightening one for him. Whatever the event, it helps to get him to talk about it. If he has had painful "shots" in the doctor's office, he may learn to get over his fear by a chance to play " 'noculation" with a teddy bear as the patient. It's important in this play that he should be the doctor—the strong one in control of everything—instead of the helpless victim. If he has had a sudden fright from a clap of thunder, he may learn to glory in a Jove-like sense of power by making a racket of his own on a tin pan. Whenever he can do the frightening thing himself instead of having it done to him, he gains a feeling of mastery.

If you are going away for a visit or must leave the house for a while, and the child seems troubled, you may be able to prevent both daytime fears and nighttime wakefulness from developing if you prepare him in advance for whatever your moves are to be. Leave him in the care only of someone he knows and trusts. Never sneak away without telling him you're going in the mistaken belief that this is less painful for all concerned. The child's faith in the world is built on his belief that under no circumstances will his parents deceive him.

As a child gets older and the fears diminish, parents can more directly encourage a child's own wish to be brave. He may surprise you by complying when he's told that from now on his calls will be answered by his parents from their own room but that they won't come to him. Arrange things so that if he feels like it he can turn on a flashlight under his pillow or sleep with his panda beside him. Show your pleasure as he makes progress. When he backslides, express confidence that he'll soon go ahead again. Get his suggestions about what might be done to make it easier for him. Let him feel you know he wants to be more independent and that you'll try to help. This more than anything will make it possible for him finally to help himself.

ALONE
AND AFRAID

It's hard for a child to be sent to bed, leaving all the pleasures of the day behind him. The closed door has a dreadful finality about it; left open, the sound of voices from the living room challenges him to listen, tempts him to get up and join the family. To make matters worse, a child, unlike most grownups, may not know how tired he is and sleep seems far away. But in spite of these obstacles most mothers do learn what conditions are most quieting for a child and what is the right mixture of indulgence and firmness about last-minute favors and good nights.

But our former friend Johnny is now two years old and, like a great many youngsters from about this age up to five or six, is troubled by small fears that at nighttime loom large. This isn't because some foolish person told him terrifying stories or because he was frightened in the dark by some accidental occurrence. It isn't because he's just "doing it for attention." Johnny's fears are for him real, though he can't tell you what they are because they're too vague and can't be put into words. It's because as a child's mental life grows more complex, familiar objects take on new meanings. Shadows assume weird shapes, wild beasts may invade the room and bite one's head off. He has no way of knowing that lions don't get into bedrooms. And there's that other, perhaps commonest of fears, that Mother might leave and never come back. Even when she promises, he feels he can't be sure. Older children can sometimes tell you what they're afraid of, but even they can't easily be argued out of it.

Johnny's mother knows both how common and how painful fears may be for small children. She knows that the answer lies neither in overindulgence nor in ruthlessly leaving him to cry it out. She must feel her way carefully, observing him in the daytime as well as at night and be willing to follow patiently what leads she gets for helping him.

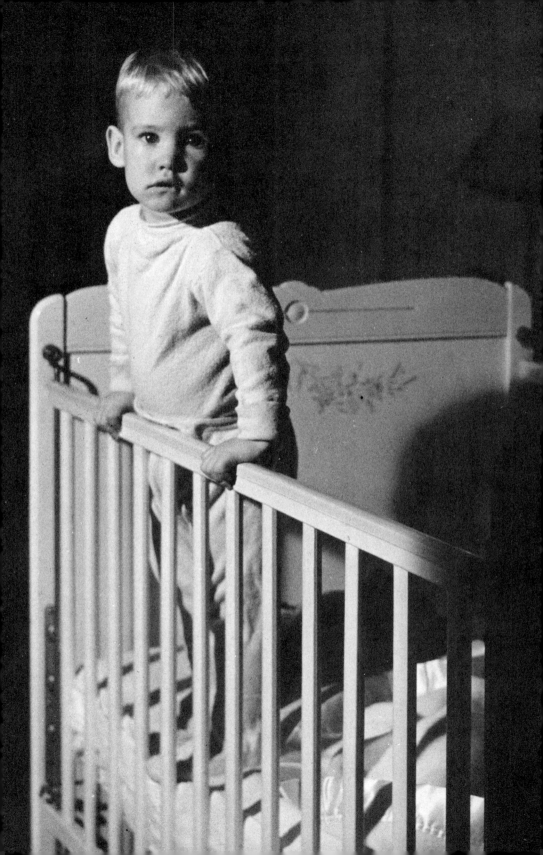

Who would think that all day long Johnny was a happy little boy full of life and funny sayings! He's had a cozy hour with Mother at the piano. But now the fatal moment has come and it's unbearable. Johnny just doesn't want to go to bed and be off by himself the whole night through. He gets into quite a panic and stalls for time, wailing, "Duck song—want duck song again." Mother explains that when he's all ready for bed they'll have the duck song once more at the piano.

*Johnny's temporarily sub-
dued but not really recon-
ciled till he's back at the
piano again. Then he for-
gets all his troubles.*

You'd never know what wailing there had been a moment ago.

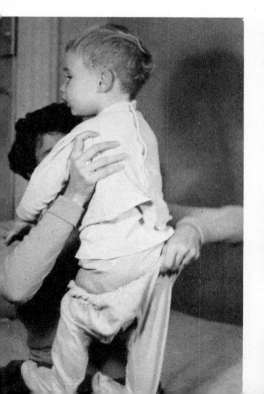

Back in his room, he knows
that now it's for keeps. He
asks for his Teddy and
Mother brings it.

"Good night, Johnny," she
says. "I'll leave your little
light on and Dad and I will
be right in the next room."

He gets a last drink of water.

Now Mother's gone and he's all alone with a long dark night ahead. He stands disconsolately for a while, but finally, being tired, will succeed in falling asleep.

At 2 A.M. Johnny wakes with a wail of anguish. Mother comes quickly. "There was a bear," he says, and she lifts him into her lap.

Mother knows that the anxious child who wakes in terror needs patient help now for future peace of mind. For about five minutes she holds him, rocks him a little, and shows him a book he likes. He's getting drowsy and she decides to put him back in his crib.

Instantly he gets tense and begins to cry. He refuses to lie down, clings to Teddy with his leg hanging over the edge of the crib in one of his favorite positions.

Mother insists that he lie down, explaining that she'll stay with him till he feels sleepier.

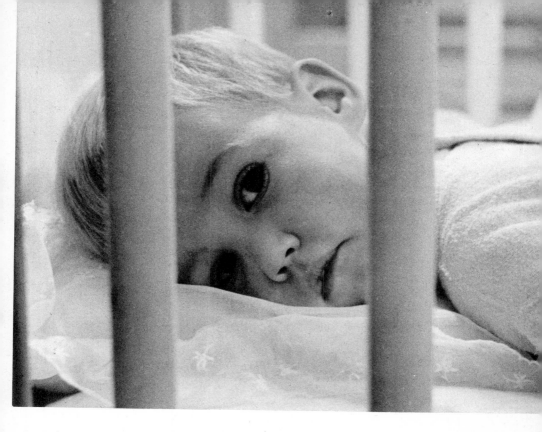

He obeys but rolls around disconsolately. Finally she will manage to tuck him in once more and pat him back to sleep.

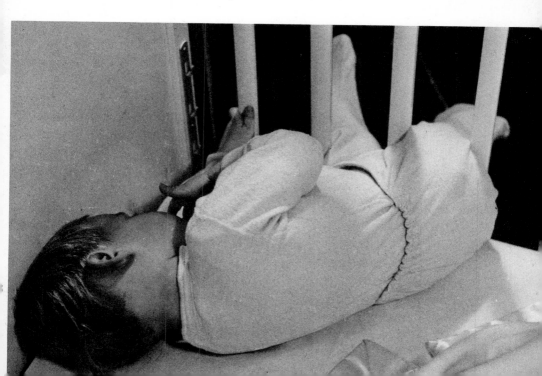

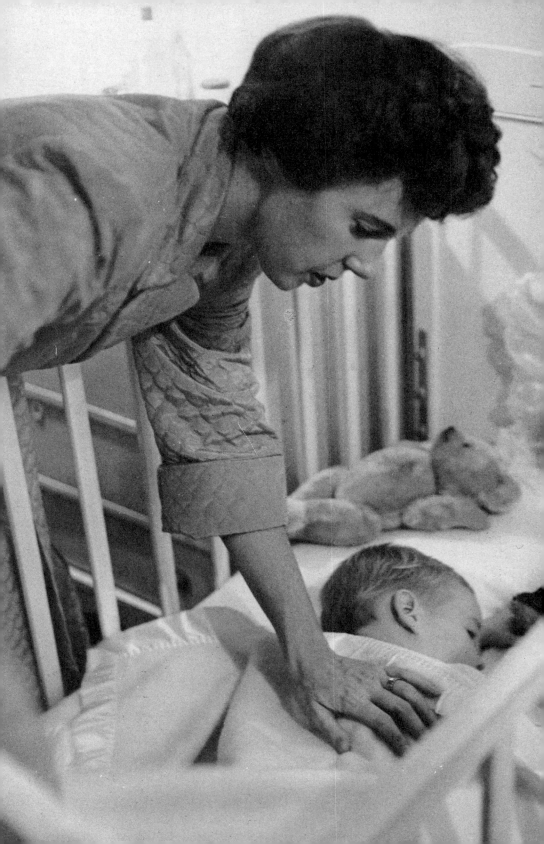

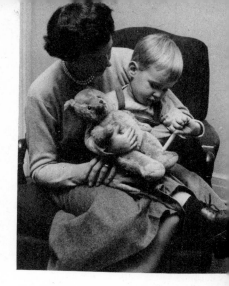

Mother hopes that, with a chance to play out daytime fears, Johnny's nighttime fears may gradually fade. Inoculations at the doctor's were an ordeal. Mother gets Johnny to play doctor, but it's important that he should be the doctor, should give instead of get the shots. Then when he thinks of the doctor, he'll tend to feel strong instead of helpless.

Mother remembers that the roaring vacuum cleaner frightened him. So when it's off she lets him play with it and turn it on again. If he hesitates she never forces him.

Johnny's always been upset when Mother goes out. So they play bye-bye-and-come-back over and over. Johnny finds he can make his mother come back and comes closer to realizing that she's never going to stay away forever.

5

When children quarrel

Children's quarrels are among Mother's worst headaches. Just as she settles to a few moments of well-earned quiet comes the shrill appeal from the next room. "Mommie—Johnny hit me—he took my——"

Must she get up and *do* something, or should children settle these things themselves?

It depends, of course; these quarrels aren't all of a kind and some are pretty harmless. Most youngsters are shockingly direct about what they want and feel. They horse around rudely; they scream at each other. They make corny cracks intended to be scathing. Loud threats of violence may finally end in kicking and shoving.

To grownups, these feuds seem senseless. They are noisy, irritating, and tiresome. But parents' nerves grow tougher as they learn to live with children. They realize that this too is part of normal growing up. And aren't some conflicts healthy, they ask themselves. Perhaps it's just as well to let all this strong feeling come tumbling out when they're young. Someday, of course, they'll have to learn to control themselves, but not all at once.

You will probably find that underneath all the rancor the children are really good friends. Threats of murder are followed soon by the gentlest of voices as two heads draw close together over a picture. Jimmy, ordinarily just plain selfish, has moments of real tenderness too. Only yesterday when the boy down the street made off with Peggy's skates, he retrieved them and handed them back to his sister with a look in his eyes that would melt your heart. The children are coming along all right, you reflect, and it's best to settle for whatever protects your own nerves and eardrums.

But there are other quarrels that go deeper, that are surprisingly painful and may leave bitterness for a lifetime. Parents learn to sense this difference in the quality of childhood conflicts. When resentments smolder and burn deep, you can't afford to be complacent. Continual teasing, surreptitious bullying, tricks to get the other fellow into trouble—such incidents, small in themselves, can often develop into something unbearable to parents and perhaps serious for the child.

To this kind of quarreling there is no simple answer. Cracking down on the bully doesn't really help; it's just born of desperation. But there are a few things parents can do. In addition, there are a good many things for them to think about that may help them look beneath the surface for what's really the matter.

First, it helps to understand that the aggressor child is really the one who needs the most help. The chances are ten to one that for all his bluster he's deeply uncertain of himself. This makes him constantly on the look-out for moments of easy power. He gets it when he snatches the toy or spoils someone else's fun. The more his parents lecture or punish, the deeper grow his doubts about himself, and the more he bullies.

Perhaps this child's first need is to know his parents are still interested in him and that he isn't an outcast. Fathers and mothers might arrange each day to spend a little time alone with such a child. Is there somewhere they might go together for a treat? How about reading together or making something they both enjoy? Or they can take time just to talk together without anyone interrupting. This investment in time and effort will probably pay off. When a child finds his parents actually like being with him, he feels better about himself, feels less urge to be quarrelsome and aggressive.

It sometimes helps to separate quarrelsome children for a while. Probably, like you, they need some privacy. If they can't have separate rooms, a special corner or just a box in which they can lock up their treasures may help. Each needs a chance to be on his own when his special friends come to the house. Perhaps a solution will be to send one child to a summer camp, or let him join a club, or go off to visit a friend or relative. There's nothing like a breathing spell for a child in this state. He needs a chance to go it alone for a bit without interference from the other.

Every child needs to know that there are some things he's good at. The quarrelsome child may be scared of rough play and of course he's secretly ashamed of being timid. Yet he may be good at swimming or something else that isn't competitive. If he can't get along with children, the friendship of a grownup may tide him over. Here's someone who likes him! By bolstering his self-respect, it actually helps him gain self-confidence. If he especially hates one of his brothers or sisters, there may be another he likes. He may be willing to do small services for this one or take actual responsibility for a younger child's care. Extra pay for extra work might help him feel he has something of real value to offer.

A child wants recognition, of course. Praise? Yes. But only if the praise is sincere and deserved. But besides these things, he probably wants his parents to share with him whatever it is that he most enjoys—comics, books, radio, TV programs—and a real hobby is a godsend.

In spite of boasting and domineering, the quarrelsome child is an unhappy child. He needs a chance to air his gripes and say just how he feels. He needs someone who'll go slow on advice, omit moral lectures, and just listen. It's always a relief to get things off your chest. It helps a lot to find your parents still like you even after they know the worst.

It's always a help to remember that with children's quarrels the child who sems to be the aggressor may not be the only offender. The charm boy of the family who wins everyone's hearts may, when your back's turned, have a subtle way of provoking another to strike the first blow. When you try to diagnose the trouble, be sure the apparent victim isn't at least partly at fault.

Of course, the best solution is to see trouble brewing and get the children doing something else before the fireworks start. Yet even when the fat's in the fire, there are still ways to put an end to things quickly. Even a bully really hopes in his heart that someone will step in and save him from himself; secretly he's grateful for it.

But when the immediate crisis has passed and there's time for reflection, parents need to take a long hard look at themselves. Have they, without realizing it, had a part to play in this state of affairs? It's easy to smile on one's lovable child. It's the other kind who taxes our unselfishness, our skill, and our patience. Fairness of course is basic. But the quarrelsome child more than any other needs time and thought. He needs someone with the insight to see his troubles. Neither indulgence nor punishment can meet the real issue. What's called for is steady, resourceful, constructive measures that help a child to live in ways that restore self-respect.

"LET ME
HAVE IT!"

A certain amount of quarreling among children is part of growing up. Young children want what they want when they want it and only gradually learn to appreciate the right of others and what it means to get along. Most childish scraps are short and sharp and soon forgotten. If the child's life as a whole is satisfying, they leave no holdovers. But sometimes, especially if one child always dominates, quarrels are surprisingly painful, leaving a sense of helplessness in the victim and guilt in the victor that may last a lifetime.

The grownup's job is to size up what goes on. If there's a fairly even give-and-take, he may do better to keep out. At other times a parent may have to intervene or, still better, try to size up what's back of the bad feeling that brings on crises. Though the underdog may need quick rescuing, it's often the aggressor whose troubles go deepest and who needs most help.

Francine, aged three, is pleased with a new jack-in-the-box. Micheline, her sister, a year older, thinks it's nice too.

"I can do it faster," says Micheline, but Francine clings to her new possession and the fight's on. Now Francie clings with both hands and tries to lie on it; Micheline grabs her round the waist and tries to pull her off.

1

Easily the victor, Micheline now graciously permits her sister to look on. Francie, helpless, tries to make the best of it. But injustice even at three is hard to take. "Let me have it," she wails, "it's mine." "I can do it better than you," says Micheline.

But promises are hard to keep once you have tasted power. Micheline goes on and on making Jack jump up, and poor Francine finds no joy at all in just watching. All she can do is suck her fingers for consolation while tears run down her cheeks. But Micheline's victory is beginning to sour. Jack doesn't quite make up for a bad conscience.

The joy of eating

There's a deep urge in all of us to feed those we love. It's fun for the young wife to please her husband with interesting new dishes. We like it when a welcome guest who drops in for a chat accepts our offer of food and drink. Greatest of all is the joy of beholding the ecstatic wriggles of your own infant or the dancing eyes of your three-year-old, aware in every fiber of his being when dinner's on the way. As he attacks it, wholly intent and unabashed, you too relax in deep content and rate eating high on the list of the pure and simple pleasures of life.

We all want to help our children experience this pleasure. We want to develop in them a firm association between food and enjoyment. This is one reason why the set feeding schedule is becoming a thing of the past and doctors advise feeding babies "on demand." This flexible plan, touched on in the first chapter, of feeding a tiny baby when he's hungry and wants to eat preserves the link of food with pleasure through the ups and downs and changes of the early days as new foods are offered and as the child's nutritional needs vary. As food continues to give him pleasure and as his attachment to those who give it grows strong, he becomes increasingly willing to accept the regular mealtime; he learns to wait for his food, knowing that it will surely come.

In spite of all this, it is not unusual to find that times come along when a child's appetite slows down. A good eater from birth sometimes grows finicky and loses some of his zest. When this happens, a real food problem may develop if mothers aren't prepared for it. If they grow anxious and start putting on too much pressure, they can easily spoil the good beginning they have made. Many children soon regain good appetites again; however, some remain slow or at least small eaters through early childhood, and yet are perfectly healthy.

As a child gets older and is ready for a three-meal-a-day schedule with a more grownup diet, the principles that make for good appetite are the same. Solid foods should be given experimentally as the baby shows he likes them. He has to get used to new tastes and, if he doesn't like them at first, it's best to wait and try again later. Mealtimes should be pleasant and satisfying. Fussing and wheedling do no good, and anxiety and nervous tension on Mother's part are quickly exploited by the child. But there's a world of difference between pressure and tactful encouragement; this is equally true when the child is no longer an infant. What's needed, is help that cheers a reluctant eater on to the finish without spoiling the pleasant relaxed atmosphere of the meal. On the other hand, when mealtime fun degenerates into high jinks and a neglected dinner plate, it's time to call quits. A child should know that mealtime is for eating and that, although he is not obliged to finish everything on his plate, he is expected to take a fair amount.

The choosiness of children about food can be the despair of inexperienced parents. Some youngsters may turn against milk itself. Or they develop an aversion to green vegetables, perhaps, or will eat no meat but frankfurters. Some may tolerate milk only if chocolate syrup is added; I have known others who insisted on smothering everything on the dinner plate with ketchup. Left to themselves, children usually get over these fads faster than you might expect, but this doesn't mean you should let them wreck the peace of the family by all sorts of special demands.

Some children are really too restless to adjust readily to the family dinner table. At this stage a child should have his meals ahead of time, in the kitchen, perhaps, where his mother is getting the family dinner, or with an older brother or sister whose companionship he enjoys. Twenty minutes or half an hour is long enough; no good purpose is served by keeping a child at table longer, if he really can't finish by then.

The poor eater can often be stimulated by a little novelty. Many a child who picks at his food will put away a big meal at a picnic. For such a youngster, "picnic supper" in the living room or even a box lunch in the back yard may give a meal that touch of glamour which the familiar dining table lacks. An amusing new dish, a flower, or a surprise under the plate when the meal has been polished off may be an incentive. Games of hunt-the-cooky often end in a triumphant child consuming the prize, and few children can resist a good big sample of their own cookery or the luncheon dish they've helped Mother prepare.

It should help mothers of slow eaters to know that the balanced diet doesn't have to be balanced at every meal or even every day. In homes where the right food is offered as a matter of course, most children get what they should have in the long run. In homes where the right food is to be had actual undernourishment is extremely rare and would be spotted by your doctor when he is giving the regular periodic checking.

But sometimes a child—even a normally good eater—stops eating suddenly. Take his temperature and report to the doctor, for this is Nature's way of telling you your child may be coming down with some illness, and, even when no other symptoms have shown up, it's a time to watch him carefully. It may be only a slight cold, but it could be something more serious.

Whatever the reasons for small appetites in otherwise healthy youngsters, they often go full steam ahead at adolescence with appetites that would astound a stevedore. Meanwhile, the main thing is to make mealtime a pleasure instead of a battleground. True, even a small baby may dawdle over a meal, or may "spit up." True, older children may develop unreasonable fads and prejudices. Still and all, the moment food becomes merely a duty there's danger of weakening the essential tie between food and pleasure which is the surest guarantee of a hearty appetite.

MORGAN LEARNS TO LIKE FOOD

At three and a half Morgan is a healthy normal boy—a bit on the thin side but wiry and active. The doctor says he's in good condition. But like many children his age, he drives his parents crazy dawdling over his food.

According to his mother, Morgan "eats practically nothing—likes only pickles," and she worries about the balanced diet she's sure he isn't getting. Worry leads to nagging and nagging to misery at mealtime.

Why should Morgan just hate food? Why must he drip tears into scrambled eggs every evening? Suddenly light dawned on his mother. She made a new resolution. She'd stop nagging; she'd find ways to make mealtimes good times.

Pancakes for Sunday breakfast. Mother readies the batter.

She invites Morgan to spoon it onto the griddle — an agreeably messy operation.

"Let's count the little bubbles," says Mother as it begins to bake, but Morgan soon loses track. When it's done Mother dashes it onto a plate with butter and syrup. "That's how Dad likes it," she says. Morgan samples it and so does Mother.

Half a pancake, a little butter, and a lot of syrup are all Morgan has for break-
fast today, but he had a good time. Later on there were no tears at the table.
Morgan just sat and talked happily except when he gave his parents funny looks,
as if to ask how long they were going to keep on leaving him alone.

It isn't manners, but syrup's good to the last drop—even better when licked from the plate. A smiling face behind it is such a new and welcome sight that Mother doesn't care.

Though Mother never nags Morgan to eat, she doesn't pretend either that eating isn't important. He helps her shell peas while she scrapes the carrots. Sometimes she pops a piece of carrot into her mouth and another into Morgan's.

He does the same with peas. He helps her with the batter for Daddy's birthday cake too. He can't resist the beater and makes the egg whites come foaming up like soapsuds.

One day they play a game called hunt the sandwich. "Finders eaters," says Mother. "Rules are that if you find where I hide it you have to eat it." Morgan finally finds it all wrapped in wax paper under the crib. Along with a hard-boiled egg, it contains strips of his favorite pickles. But he eats it because that's the rule.

The change in Morgan—which came gradually—didn't depend on doing these particular tricks with food or on any other tricks. There aren't any sure "techniques" for getting children to enjoy their food and liking to eat. Nearly everything depends on the atmosphere and on the attitudes of the people around them, on their being willing to indulge some of a child's vagaries but knowing how to keep them within the bounds of good sense.

Not every mother, of course, can make the changes in herself that Morgan's mother made. If you're the anxious type, it's not easy to stop being anxious. But you can try; and if you're not too bad a case, maybe you'll succeed. Eventually Morgan became a fairly good eater, a real pleasure to have at the table. He still likes pickles.

1

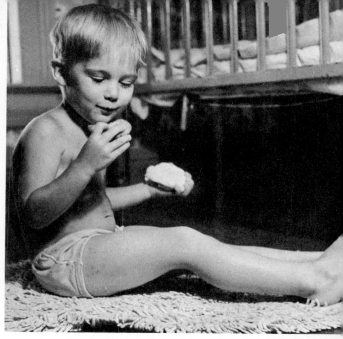

The importance
of being Father

Fortunately we've left behind the type of father who growls behind his newspaper and thinks of home mainly as a place where he puts up his feet and rests. Nowadays even fathers who spend most of their time in offices work around home a lot, too. They repair equipment, keep grounds in order, and sometimes even build their own houses. Almost inevitably the children tag along and learn to work with them. But even today, it's sometimes hard for a father to see as much of his children as he'd like to. Work keeps him away late, he may be in military service, he may have to travel a good deal, and it's easy to lose touch with the children and their needs. Meanwhile Mother is around all day and is on hand to make so many minor decisions which seem important to the child. Father comes home to find that Lucy isn't to go to Jean's house for a while and Paul is to be allowed to stay up tonight until nine. He is all at sea until it is explained to him that Lucy would be risking exposure to scarlet fever at Jean's and that Paul has been promised he may help Mother make his space suit for the party.

Yet children, whether they're boys or girls, need to feel both parents as active forces in their daily lives from the moment they're born. Fathers add very special ingredients to their children's emotional diet and, if these are left out, children miss something vital.

While Mother represents the home and the ordering of all its details, Father represents the outside world where there are important jobs to be done; where people go to far off places, meet strangers, and earn money so families can have homes. This world in which Father moves so easily is an everlasting challenge to the child's thirst for adventure. Most fathers are very aware of the grownup world their children will face some day and want to start right now preparing their youngsters. When a father combines this kind of realistic toughness with understanding and tenderness, a child is indeed lucky.

A boy looks to his father for leadership. His own maturing goes 12 forward more surely if he has tested his father's superior wisdom and respects it. What form this leadership will take depends, of course, on the man himself. Some fathers have mechanical skills that a boy can learn if he watches closely. Others have no mechanical gift and as household handyman they may be woefully lacking. If so, they may have some other talent or interest which they can share. In any case, a boy should find his father a friend and counselor, someone who isn't overpowering to a small child, yet goes about life with a certain strength and assurance. This lays the groundwork for manly growth in his sons.

A little girl needs to sense in her father that he is happy to have a daughter. More than anything else this will make her glad, too, that she is a girl. This awareness of her femininity and its special value for him will give her dignity and value in her own eyes and presently she begins to accept with joy the prospect of one day being a mother. All this helps build a sound foundation for successful relations to the masculine half of the human race.

Although the major part of the care of small children inevitably falls to the mother, a real relationship between a father and his sons and daughters can be very soon established. It is best done by knowing them and sharing their care from the very beginning. The whole family gains when it's Father who takes a turn at changing the diaper, at warming and giving the bottle, or handling tempers. Sometimes it falls to him to demand that youngsters cut out their bickering or tune down the radio or go to bed when they're told. Just as today's father is no longer the dispenser of punishment to young sinners when he comes home in the evening, so too he doesn't just yell for help from Mother. He manages his share of periodic crises. Like Mother, he too will listen to childhood woes and find ways to soothe them. When father has been given the chance to know and enjoy his children from the time they're born, he need never suffer the experience of suddenly feeling, later on, that he's face to face with a young stranger of five, or fourteen—or perhaps twenty.

Mother can do much to promote a father's good relation to his children. He'll need not only the chance to take charge now and then. He must be able to count on his wife's wholehearted support of his judgment and authority too. There are bound to be some differences in the
ways two parents approach some matters. If disagreements go deep, they

have to be talked over thoroughly and a compromise course agreed on. Both parents must be aware that there's more than one right way of managing children and that in whatever they decide they can count on each having the backing of the other.

FINDING TIME
FOR FOUR CHILDREN

Like most family breadwinners, Ned is busy all day away from home. His work on the research staff of a university is exacting and he often gets home late, his mind still occupied with problems of the day. He might like time to relax and do as he pleases, and he certainly wants time to enjoy the company of his wife now and then. But there's Michael and John, Kathy and David, who are right there with a thousand matters on *their* minds, and Ned wants to hear what they have to say too. Sometimes it seems as though there isn't a split second for him to turn around; one or another youngster or perhaps all of them come swarming in on him. But he knows that the time to get to know his children is now and that this goes for the baby as well as eight-year-old Michael. He suspects that watching them develop may be worth a little bedlam during the short years before they're all grown up and take off for goodness knows where.

Late in those rare evenings when Ned isn't working and is finally alone with his wife, she brings him up to date on the youngsters' doings. Each child is a very definite personality and this inevitably means special problems. How to do the best by each one? How can they as parents best contribute to their children's sound emotional growth? How can they help four strenuous young individualists accept each other? Sometimes Ned and his wife differ, but they can always discuss their differences, and out of the talks come clearer understanding, wiser plans for action. They are equal partners in the greatest project in the world.

"*The best men are cooks!*" *In this family Sunday morning's the time when Ned and the children make pancakes de luxe while Mother attends to David, eight months. When it's Kathy's turn at the beater, Michael and John are polite but inwardly feel superior.*

Each new baby's altogether different from the others, thinks Ned. David has long talks with his father on important matters.

Mike and John make a Kon-Tiki *like the raft in the book they all loved. Ned lets them work along at their own speed. The finished job is important, but fun in the making is equally so.*

When life gets too hectic a good sing is more than likely to have a quieting effect. Mother starts by herself—others join when and if they want to.

Baseball, of course, and it's apt to be punctuated by arguments about whose turn it is and all that. Ned is a patient, impressive umpire. In most families there's one among the children who finds it harder than others to abide by rules of the game.

Active sport isn't Ned's favorite pastime, but it's worth it to hear the wham of the ball and to see the eager stance of the young batter—his own son.

Ned has such wonderful ideas. Here's fun with old snapshots.
The boys can hardly believe that big solemn baby was actually
their father. Later they help get the car ready for a trip to see
the Yankee double header with the Browns.

Biggest thrill of all is a trip to Ned's laboratory. He knows how to handle even dangerous things safely and he painstakingly shows Michael and John how, too.

It's John's birthday and his friends have come for cake in the yard. Ned gets home just in time.

With the men elsewhere, Kathy and her mother stretch out with a book together —and to enjoy a bit of woman talk.

Later, while Mother gets dinner, Ned takes over. Sons are terrific, but a little daughter is extra-special, and Ned and Kathy both know it.

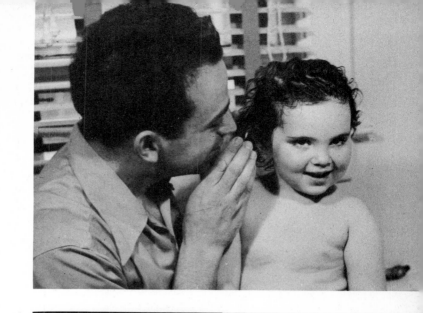

Evening—and the younger children are tucked in bed. But are they? Here's Kathy full of good reasons for having come downstairs again.

Crossword puzzles are relaxing. Michael and John may look on quietly, even help a little till their bedtime.

A quiet house at last—just the two of them. It's like heaven.

Give grandparents a place in your child's life

What place have grandparents in your child's life? Is it possible for old and young to really enjoy each other? That depends on the grandparents, you may answer. True enough, but a half truth. Not only grandparents but parents too must be ready to do their share to help bridge the gap between the generations.

Your own private state of mind about your own or your husband's parents will be quickly sensed by a child and will count heavily. If you think older people are just a bore to be put up with now and then, so will your children. No matter how hard you try to hide your feelings, they will know by contagion and will almost surely betray you by being rude and unfriendly. But if you habitually think of older people as both interesting and human and count them among your friends, then your children will follow suit and be far more likely to find common ground with their grandparents. There's also plenty you can actually *do* to bring this about.

"We hope you'll get out that old set of barnyard animals when Chuck and Billy come; I used to adore it when I was little," wrote one mother, just before a trip to the grandparental home. Or, "The kids are just wild for a plastic wading pool. You wanted to know what they'd like. I guess that's it."

"The baby's shy," said another. "Just don't pay any attention to him at first. If you let him alone, he'll come round in his own time. And oh yes, I better warn you! Mary *hates* to be asked if she likes her teacher and Ted can't bear hearing what a big boy he's grown to be! Just plunge right in and show them what you've got in the house." Grandmother's kitchen or Grandfather's workshop or office are pretty sure to interest children, especially if they make something there themselves. Shopping expeditions (loot for the child, of course) have special thrills.

When grandparents arrive for a visit, make your plans ahead of time so as to get things off to a good start. For instance, you can maneuver them at once to look at the pet mice, or the new truck, or the family of dolls. As a substitute for those polite boring pleasantries in the living room, this quick approach to the child's own world is sure to pay off.

Remembering your own childhood, you'll know what games and stunts you used to enjoy when *you* were young. At moments of tension these come in handy. Youngsters are delighted at tales of their parents' early naughtiness, especially of how they got punished; or the time they fell off the woodshed and had to have stitches taken; or what happened when the whole family had measles. If you can get these yarns going, the oldsters will take their cues.

If grandparents live nearby, there are many practical jobs they may be able to do, such as sitter services. In emergencies they may be indispensable, and everything is easier when the children and Grandmother are old friends. Even when grandparents live far away, there are the letters, the birthday presents, the snapshots, the funny postcards or drawings, the small unexpected gift for no reason at all to send and receive. This way, grandparents are still important members of the family, are in the air, as it were, and are part of the magic circle.

Then there are parties. Wherever did we get the notion that parties must always be held according to age groups? Family jambories, especially those on Christmas and anniversaries, have a special flavor and meaning when young and old share the preparations and the pleasures. Grandparents aren't just for practical chores and emergencies. You can have fun with them too!

Children will discover, of course, that in some ways grandparents are different. They "look old," perhaps. Often they can't run, don't like sudden loud noises; they may have to rest awhile every day; they worry more than parents about children getting into danger or falling and hurting themselves. This can be explained to children very directly. "Older people can't bear as much noise as we can. They're inclined to worry. When I'm old, I'll probably be that way about *your* children." Grandparents can do their own explaining too. "You see," they may say, "I just *can't* run after you; so when I'm taking care of you and you want to go somewhere out of sight, you *must* tell me about it *first*."

Occasionally there are difficult, even "impossible," grandparents, those who play favorites, for example, or complain constantly of the children's behavior. Letting grandparents "spoil" the children, though it may be inconvenient, isn't nearly as destructive as those rancorous arguments with the parents on how the children should be managed. Parents must hold fast to their own authority, even if it comes to a showdown. This isn't always easy, but frank words can sometimes clear the atmosphere, especially when each side is willing to listen and learn as well as talk. Sometimes you'll need to talk things over frankly with a child too. If he has been inconsiderate and rude and is old enough to know better, he can be held to certain standards. But perhaps his grandparent was at fault. "Yes, I think Grandmother was wrong about that," you may say when a child's complaint is just. "I know how you must have felt about it."

As a new grandmother myself, I am realizing that we of the oldest generation must be prepared to give generously of our time and interest. Every child welcomes a person who he knows will really play with him, and we'd better learn how. But we must also come to grips with the primary fact that the youngsters are our children's children, not our own. We must guard against our own unconscious efforts to stage a last-ditch attempt to reassert our former authority in a struggle over the youngest generation. The truly wise grandparent is aware of this pitfall and is on guard. We must be fully aware that young parents can run their own lives and families very well indeed and that basic to good relations with them is an honest respect for their decisions and opinions, even when they differ from our own. We must also be constantly aware that even when ties of affection are strong, young families need to be by themselves. From time to time we must know how to fade out of the picture gracefully— and without resentment. We'll do this best if our own lives are busy and interesting and include work and friends of our own.

But it's you, the parents, who hold the trump cards. The children are yours. At any moment, you can be self-sufficient. You no longer really need your parents as they need you. Remember, then, that old people dread loneliness. They don't want to be merely tolerated, no matter how tactfully. They want to feel needed and useful. No matter how busy they are, their own daily doings are never a real substitute for the warm joy that comes of serving one's very own, and they yearn to recapture this joy through the new lives that are coming along. Knowing this should make you generous, fully aware of the crucial part you have to play in bringing out the best or the worst in both the older and younger generations. Young parents must be quick, for example, to sense which jobs will be too back-breaking or too nerve-wracking. They will resist the temptation to demand services merely to suit their own convenience. At the same time they will gladly accept, wherever they can, whatever their elders really want to give.

All of us perhaps succumb too easily to the ready-made notion that children are best off when they spend as much time as possible with other youngsters. Too often it is assumed that the most age can expect of youth is to be polite and respectful. Do we perhaps cheat our children when we rule out older people as active forces in their lives? Are we impoverishing their lives if we deprive them of a more secure world where they belong not only to a family but to a whole clan as well?

In the past, old and young, given the chance, have found deep wisdom in each other. Can today's parents rediscover for their children the particular vein of riches that lies in a warm relationship with the oldest generation? Parents, here's a challenge to your maturity.

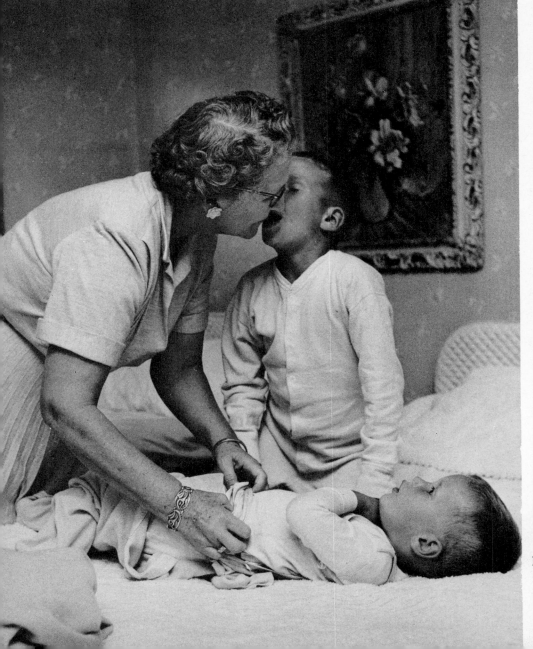

STEVEN AND ROSS
GO VISITING

"We're going visiting!" Steven, aged five, and Ross, two and a half, have been telling their friends about it for days. Their parents are going away in the car to spend a week with old college friends in a distant town and the children will go to their grandparents, who live four miles away. They weren't sure at first how they'd like it. "Why couldn't Mom and Dad take us along?" wailed Steven. "Goodness," said Granny, "don't you suppose they ever want to get rid of you two rapscallions!" There was always a smile under Granny's serious face that made children like her. They liked her house, too, where they went often and had even stayed overnight and where Dad had lived when he was a little boy. Their grandparents also often came to visit them, and they'd all been old friends from as long as they could remember.

Mother's busy getting both the house and her clothes in order before she leaves. The children try to help; Mother pauses in her ironing to explain a picture to Steven.

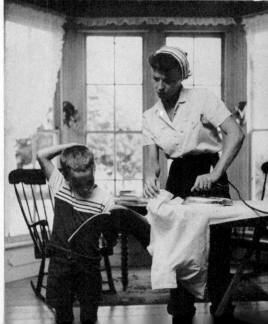

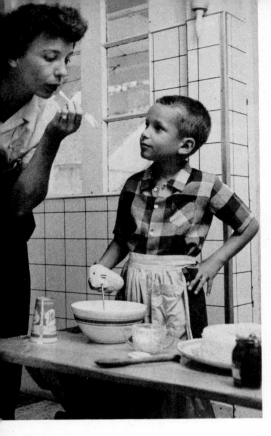

The day has come and the grand-parents are expected in time for lunch. Early in the afternoon the children will start off with them for their house and Dad and Mom will go their way. Steven's baking a cake as a present for Granny and Grand-dad to take home. When it's all done, Ross helps with the cherry decora-tions, but Steven insists on placing the last one. When the grandparents arrive, he carries it triumphantly into the living room.

A gift for someone you love makes the giver happy, too, especially when you make it yourself. "It's our favorite kind of cake," says Steven. "That's funny," says Grandma, "it just happens to be our favorite too."

They take them to visit the two new sheep Dad brought home. Later, while Ross shows Granddad his treasures, Steven whispers that he wants ice cream with chocolate sauce for dinner.

Last-minute consultation. "And don't worry if Ross doesn't eat very much," says Mother. Favorite toys are packed to go along.

Grandma's stricter than Mother about table manners, but the children are used to it.

They love helping Granddad in his shop.

*The children think it's wonderful to have a granny who paints and like to watch
her at her easel. "I'm no Michelangelo," she says, "but it sure takes my mind
off my troubles better than cooking or knitting." Steven and Ross don't quite
understand this remark, but they think the pictures are beautiful. Sometimes
Granny gives them brushes and paints of their own and lets Steven mix up a lot
of colors. Ross is too young, she says, but she lets him dip his brush in water and
"paint" a big piece of paper.*

Granny pays more attention than Mother does to even the slightest scratch. She gets out disinfectants and bandages and goes right to work. Ross is enjoying all this and likes to show off his bandage.

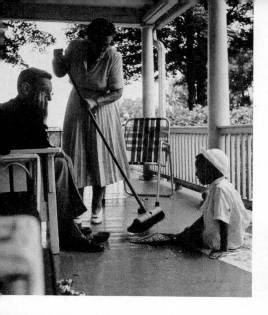

She's neater than Mother too. Before lunch or supper everything has to be cleared up.

But she also lets them play much longer—reading their favorite stories over and over. They can make going to bed take a long time, especially if they get Grandma talking about times when Daddy was a little boy "and used to sleep in this very bed in this very room."

But Grandma gets quite angry when Ross goes running away. If he does it when her back's turned he can be quite far away before Granny sees him, and she has to go puffing after him. Ross has tried it before and it makes him feel bigger than Steven or even Granny to be able to tease her this way.

But Granny catches up with him and brings him back. "Never, never do that again," she says.

It's been a wonderful week at their grandparents' home with lots of things to do. Most wonderful of all is the day when Mom and Dad come back. So much to tell them about! Everybody talks at once.

All tuckered out, but well worth it! How do their parents ever stand it day in and day out? they wonder. Steven maybe. But that Ross! He's a regular little demon! Bright as a button, though—doesn't miss a trick. Never did like children who were too good. The house will be quiet without them, but wonderfully restful too. Now they can put things to rights again and look forward to long lovely hours of just going about their own business.

Another baby in the family

A new baby in the family is an event that stirs many emotions in an older child. So far he's had things pretty much his way and has basked in the warmth of a genial family spotlight playing on him rather steadily. His feelings at the prospect of a new baby will probably be a mixture of pleasure, pride, anxiety, and curiosity, but there may also be downright resentment openly expressed. After the initial excitement, these confused emotions often collapse into boredom. "What's all the fuss about?" the older child seems to ask.

But the doubts keep cropping up. "Will that silly old baby want my fire engine?" he wonders. He may begin to make all sorts of special demands on Mother, have unaccountable moods of sulking, or take to clowning. But, in spite of these conflicting currents, most children are, on the whole, pleased with the idea of a new baby, and their parents' delight in the coming event is contagious. When the baby has arrived they're proud, especially if they find that all the reassuring small events of daily life keep on as usual. It is the parents' task to see that as nearly as possible they do.

It helps to tell a child about the baby ahead of time and include him in all the delightful preparations. Two or three months ahead may be time enough for a younger child, but it does no harm to remember that even small children have an uncanny nose for news. Veiled remarks of grownups arouse suspicions and even anxieties. Hearing the facts straight from their parents gives children a chance to say what's on their minds so that confusions can be cleared up.

If this is the child's first experience in welcoming a newcomer to the family, it will almost certainly call forth some questions about how babies come, and it is one of the natural moments to tell him what he wants to know. A simple straightforward explanation may run something like this: "Your new brother or sister is growing inside Mother's body in a special place made just for a baby to grow in. It's called the uterus and is the same place where *you* grew during that time we were so happy to know you were coming. What fun we all had getting your clothes ready just as we're doing now for the new baby! You were so cute, too, when you finally came! But you were very tiny and couldn't walk or talk or do anything for yourself at first. Later, of course, babies get big; they turn into children who can run around and ride a bike and walk to the corner store by themselves and do errands, just the way you can now."

Often this amount of explanation will satisfy a child at this stage, and there is no advantage in forcing on him more than he seems ready to take. However, children's curiosity advances rapidly. Depending on a child's age and interests, he may next ask how the baby gets out of Mother, and a straightforward answer is still best. It might go something like this: The womb or uterus where the baby grows has a way of pushing the baby down and out when the right time comes. Mother has an opening between her legs which stretches to let the baby come through. She goes to the hospital for this, so that a doctor and nurse will be there to help the baby come out.

The best time to tell a child about birth is when he really seems to want to know. This may be before a new baby is on the way or it may not be until after the baby is born. But parents should be alert to the unspoken as well as the spoken question and shouldn't risk missing their cues. Once a child senses that his parents are putting him off, he will begin to feel that this subject is somehow taboo and he'd better keep off it too.

Days, weeks, even months may pass, but sooner or later children are likely to spring another question—how did the baby get into Mother. Parents, of course, are bound to differ in the ease with which they can discuss such things. The whole subject of sex education is overloaded with feelings fostered by the kind of world we live in and the kind of childhood each of us has had. But a child can understand the main facts if you tell them simply and if, from the beginning, you have used definite words for every part of the body, male and female. It's certainly better too for him to learn about sex from you. It helps him feel that the door is always open between him and his parents and that they are glad to have him ask them whatever he wants to know.

But the new baby may be a cause not only for curiosity but for anxiety. A child may well be troubled if his mother disappears without warning, in the night perhaps, when the times comes that she goes to the hospital. Perhaps he already knows that hospitals are for sick people and that sick people sometimes die. Could the new baby make his mother die and stay away from him forever? This is a fearful thought.

It helps to let a child see the hospital ahead of time, if only from the outside. You want him to think of it as a familiar and comfortable place. His parents can tell him where the mother's room will be and explain that she won't really be sick, but wants to rest after the baby is born. She will miss him, of course, and will come back to him as soon as she can— about the same amount of time it takes between last Sunday and next Sunday.

Whoever takes care of a child while his mother is away should be someone he knows well—his father, grandmother, a friend he is used to and trusts, someone who understands the family routines and will carry on with no more dislocations than necessary. The child needs to be told who this will be in time to get used to the prospect.

Soon after the baby comes he'll be glad to hear Mother's familiar voice on the phone. Small remembrances, notes, and messages can carry the reassuring knowledge that she is well, that she cares, that she will come back.

The day the new baby is actually brought home is greeted by most children with excitement rivaled only by Christmas. They'll want to hold the baby and learn how he looks and feels. They delight in tiny fingers and toes and in funny grimaces. With a little supervision they learn to cuddle and care for the baby. Bath time is great fun and gives children a chance to see the naked baby as a complete little person. If it's a boy, a mother may want to explain that all little boys and grown men too have a penis. If it's a sister it may be a good time to say that girls and grown women are different from the very beginning. How much she'll want to say depends on what the child wants to know.

But after the first excitement, some children lose their first intense interest. To them, the baby seems disappointingly small and helpless, hardly worth all the fuss. And fuss there is bound to be, not only on the part of parents, but on the part of all the friends and relatives who flock in. It may be wise to postpone the rush of visitors a day or so. This will give the older child the feeling that he can settle back into his old familiar life and that the family circle isn't too different from what it's always been.

More than ever, after the advent of a new baby in the home, an older child needs the assurance of his parents' continuing interest in him. They mustn't neglect to show their love for the baby either, of course; their welcome to the newcomer is one way of helping the older child feel the same way. But constant cooings and admiring comment over the new baby, to the neglect of the older child, are well calculated to start things off on the wrong foot. Friends, visitors, relatives can all help this situation by co-operating. A little praise, an affectionate glance or comment, some time alone to play with him or read to him just as you always did —all these will help him to know that in spite of changes, he too always has the place in the heart of the family he always had.

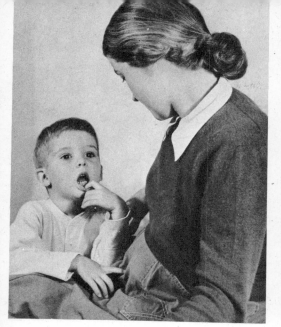

MORGAN
GETS A SISTER

Here's Morgan again. You've met him twice before—once as a two-year-old on a ladder at the playground, and once stalling over his food. Now he's a big boy of four and has just learned there's to be a great event in the family—a new baby. For a long time he's wanted a big brother; now Mother tells him he can *be* a big brother to either a little brother or sister, but no one knows which. "Where is she?" Morgan asks, and Mother says the baby is growing inside her body and will come out after a while. "If I listen, perhaps I can hear him crying," says Morgan.

Mother explains that the baby isn't big enough yet to come out but that Morgan can help her get his own old crib ready for the baby and sort out his baby clothes. Once he too was a tiny little newborn baby and wore tiny little clothes hardly any bigger than a doll's. Morgan listens, then all of a sudden loses interest entirely. He wants Mother to read him his favorite story and curls up on the couch beside her cozily. She realizes that he needs the feeling that life isn't going to be altogether different and that he can go on being as important to her and Dad as ever.

One day Mother introduces him to Irene, who is coming to stay with him for a few days while she is in the hospital having the baby. Dad, of course, will be with him too, but Irene will get lunch for him and help while Dad is away at the office. Irene is lots of fun. She knows some wonderful games and can tell jokes. All three of them have a lot of fun together and Irene knows just how to help him out of his snow pants. He is so sorry when she leaves that Irene has to promise she'll come again for a little visit even before the baby is born.

Mother will go over with Irene just what she has told Morgan about the baby, the hospital, and the doctor. She will tell her that she believes in being entirely truthful about whatever he wants to know. She will explain, too, that questions are unpredictable and that sometimes a child is a little anxious about where Mother is, whether she's really coming back, and what a new baby in the family will mean to him. She'd like Irene to talk over anything that puzzles her with Morgan's father—or with her when she comes back.

It's fun to help with painting, and Morgan and Mother spend a happy morning making the crib fresh and lovely.

He just can't believe he was ever tiny enough to sleep comfortably in that crib.

*One morning Morgan wakes
to find a present for him on
the bed. It's from Mother—
and he at once suspects that
the big moment has come.*

*"It's a little sister and her name's Austine," says Dad,
coming in at that moment, and gives Morgan an extra-big
hug. "Later on we'll talk to Mother on the telephone."*

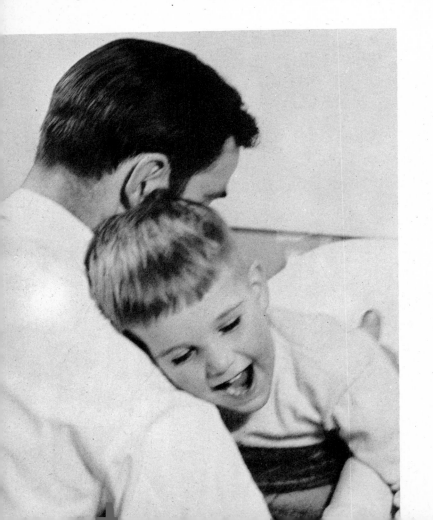

1

7   *Morgan and Dad get breakfast together, and this morning Dad has plenty of time to sit around talking and blowing smoke rings.*

The telephone rings and there's Mother. "How's my big boy?" she says. "I love you, Morgan."

Later Irene shows him how to play the harmonica. They plan a surprise for Dad's supper.

A few days later Morgan helps Dad collect the clothes for Austine to wear home from the hospital. "The smallest blue sacque," says Mother's list. Dad guesses she must mean this one.

On the day that Mother comes home, Morgan rushes out, grabs her hand, and pulls her to the house. Dad follows with a bunch of blankets. Perhaps there's no baby after all!

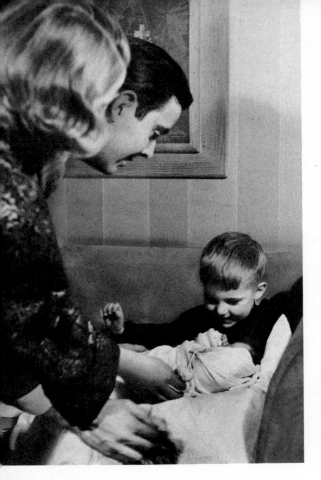

"Is she alive?" Morgan asks when Austine, wearing the blue sacque, is put in his lap. Then Austine yawns and he giggles. She looks queer, not a bit the way he expected.

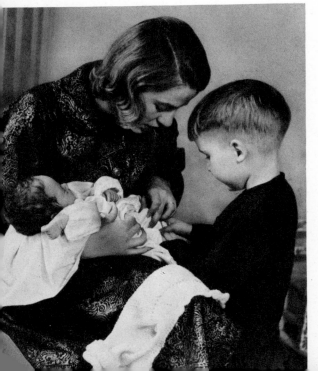

"I want to see what she looks like," says Morgan. Mother shows him the baby's tiny hands and feet. "Tomorrow when she gets her bath you can see her all over," she says.

17

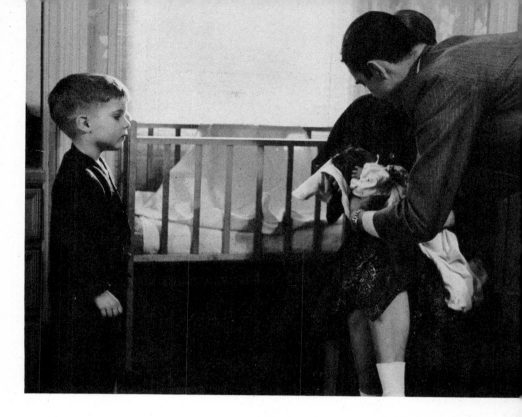

Morgan's not quite sure after all how he feels about having a perfect stranger in his crib. He crawls under, makes baby sounds, pretending he can't walk or talk and devouring crackers.

Morgan can see Mother nurse Austine if he likes. But, knowing it's hard for him, she wisely doesn't make much show of it. He still devours crackers for consolation and wonders a lot about people's bodies—about the difference between boys and girls, grownups and children.

"Look at my *nipples," he says suddenly.*

Before Austine came, Morgan used to feed himself, but now he wants to be fed. Mother will let him be babyish for a day or so but will gradually ease him back to his former independence.

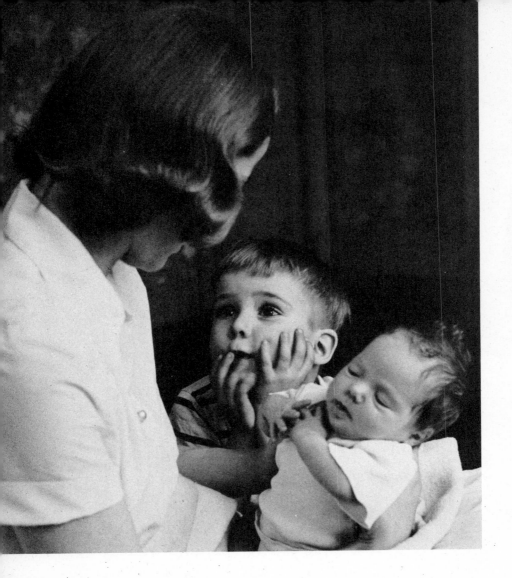

In the days that follow, Morgan tries all sorts of tricks to make sure that Mother's still there when he wants her. Once in a while he wakes up at night and calls; sometimes he has fits of giggles and silliness, talks baby talk, gets sudden tempers, and cries more easily. But most of the time he seems peaceful and goes about his daily business as before. Sometimes he likes to watch while Mother bathes or dresses Austine, but often, too, he pushes himself between them. He wants Mother to pay attention just to him and forget that silly old baby.

But actually Morgan can't help liking Austine. His doubts fade as he finds his parents keep on caring for him just the same. The really important things haven't changed.

Helping him get well

When I was a child and the clinical thermometer soared to 101, 102, 103 degrees or more, I was put to bed, my mother erected a card table nearby and at once set out a little dispensary. Medicines, temperature charts, and other nursing paraphernalia took their places in a neat row. Books and flowers, games and puzzles somehow appeared beside them in a jiffy, and my mother herself settled in a nearby chair with knitting, sewing, household accounts, or correspondence transferred to my room. The rest of the family, especially my father, used to laugh as they poked their heads in.

"Mother just loves it when somebody in the family's sick," they said.

"Not at all," said my mother indignantly. "I just think when someone's sick it should be done right."

She did do it right and to tell the truth did enjoy it a little too—not enough to make us want to stay sick, but enough so that each one of us when it was our turn felt delightfully indulged and special and peaceful inside. I am not talking of very long or serious illness of course; that's quite another matter. But children need this feeling of being special now and then; they need it so much that the child who is never sick often feels left out.

Right at the beginning of an illness, a child needs some brief information about himself so he'll know what to expect within the next week or so. It's best to explain what's being done to make him get well and how he can do his share to help. The more explicit you can be, the better. Sometimes children get the idea that they're sicker than they are and they will need a clear account from their parents, or the doctor. Vague comments intended to be reassuring can actually be alarming and whispered conferences with the doctor in the next room or phone conversations in a lowered voice with friends may start a child worrying.

Parents should be ready for the tedious period of convalescence with some very tangible resources. Sometimes a grown-up friend of Mother's whom the child especially likes might be glad to come and play with him 1 for an hour to act as relief while Mother snatches some sleep. The child's own young friends may come too, singly and for limited amounts of time. Brother and sister too may take turns at being nurse. Now's the time to explore the top shelf of the closet for those surplus presents from last Christmas which were put away for just such an occasion and which may now be brought out singly. It's the time too for Mother to revise long-forgotten skills of her own. There are all those endless possibilities with scissors and paper, the lovely "snow flakes" or strings of dolls that appear miraculously by cutting snips from folded paper,—then *un*folding it. Scrap books, we remember, can be made from notebooks by pasting in pictures from magazines or old greeting cards. Homemade sewing cards are easily made by tracing an animal or other outline picture on a piece of card-board, then punching large holes all around it with a knitting needle. There are lots of possibilities here for the child to get ready his holiday gifts for friends or family.

Then there are simple amusements like soap bubbles blown from an old spool; if you dip one end in soapy water you can blow through the other. Or you may want to introduce your patient to the mysteries of carbon paper—he'll enjoy tracing the outline of some picture. A small mirror can make beams of sunlight dance about the room; or a magnet pressed against the underside of a box lid can magically guide a needle about on the top. Dime stores hold endless resources. Paper-doll or cow-boy cutouts can occupy children for hours. There are games and puzzles for all ages, small plastic dollhouse furniture, cars, animals, and handi-craft material. A new album of children's records, both songs or stories, may hit the spot, especially if there's also a small bedside record player so the child can put them on and take them off himself. These, of course, are also good long-term investments along with the indispensable picture books.

The convalescent child needs to be made comfortable in bed. A board or even a small chair across the end of the bed under the mattress can be made to support his head. He may need something firm at the bottom to brace his feet against. A pillow under his knees often helps. Better than the standard bed table is the board or dining-table leaf sup-ported across his bed on chair backs at a comfortable height; and he will need a large box or box lid with high sides in which to keep miscellaneous objects from falling all around and getting lost.

If medicine is a problem and no diet interferes, pills may go down more easily embedded in a marmalade sandwich or a maraschino cherry; liquid sucked through a colored straw is likely to be more fun than when drunk from a cup. If something tastes really bad, chunks of ice held in the mouth just before and again just after swallowing the bad-tasting stuff deaden the sense of taste.

As for food, a "picnic" box with small wrapped sandwiches or other surprises may add new appeal to familiar food. Or perhaps you'll butter a piece of toast and cut it into odd shapes for the patient to fit together jigsaw fashion before eating. A "face" may be made on a slice of buttered toast by sifting a cinnamon and sugar mixture onto it through a stencil and setting it for a moment in a hot oven. Or you may ask the child to guess what he'll find on the bottom of his glass plate when he's finished his food. Beforehand, you will have pasted a funny picture on the under side or drawn one yourself with nail polish.

Knowing what to expect of yourself, too, will make things easier. Each of us must reckon on our own emotional and physical limitations. If kind friends have stepped forward with offers of help, accept with pleasure; and be glad when a husband can share the job or take over for a while. Every mother of a sick child will do her job better if she can manage to get a change of scene and atmosphere for a short period each day. This will help her stay fit for the long haul. And it isn't only the convalescent who needs her. She's likely to discover that her other children too have a fatal propensity for getting into scrapes and unhappiness just when it's least convenient. They also are entitled to their fair share of Mother. One way of keeping them fit is helping them to realize from the start just why sickness in the family makes special demands on her and just how they can help. Thus even small brothers and sisters can play a vital part in bringing a sick child back to health, learning to pull their weight as part of their own intimate family circle.

Much as we all dread illness for our children, mothers sometimes make the discovery that in some mysterious way—if the illness is mild— it seems to improve a child's state of mind. In spite of the discomfort, the boredom, and the moments of despondency, a child is often his best and most loving self while he is ill. "Such a good patient!" is our way of putting it. We were afraid he might get spoiled by all the gifts and the special attentions he got, yet with just the usual common-sense planning and gradual easing of him back to his normal routines again he quickly became his old active and independent self. Even more, he may have gained a certain peace and serenity. Why is this?

Perhaps you may come to the conclusion that as a parent you yourself were different during the illness. Giving to your child generously of yourself has made you feel closer than ever before—and this sense of closeness satisfies a long-felt need. It isn't that you ever neglected him, but, like most parents, you were so busy that you hardly realized how many fine things that might have been part of your relationship got crowded out by the steady round of daily duties. Now you realize that while your child was ill you let a lot of household chores go with a clear conscience. You canceled dates, you devoted yourself to your child. When friends telephoned, they were considerate of the fact that a sick child needed his mother and they didn't keep you talking so long.

As for the games and toys and treats, they were fun, of course—but largely as a symbol that people cared. What was even better was that you all shared the play and the fun. There were those long "conversations," while Mother or Father just sat in a chair by the bed in the late afternoon and forgot to turn the lights on and told stories and riddles and laughed with the child. These hours added to the sense of closeness.

How many of these unexpected values can be made to last in normal times? Mothers can't always neglect their chores, or stop seeing their friends. Once a child is well, he must learn to adjust himself to the life of the household and others around him. Yet, if you are a busy mother, you know too that for months on end you may have been running in a groove, scarcely noticing when one or another child was getting short shrift. When a child needed something obvious, you were right there, of course; it was the subtler but no less important needs that went by the board. Yet, after all, you now realize your children are more important than a spotless house; you might, if you set your mind to it, revise some standards, putting first things first so that you can still find time just to enjoy a child's company now and then.

In these ways something of the generosity and wholeheartedness and sharing that went on in the family during the time your child was sick can perhaps be salvaged. If so, sickness in your family has been an experience through which everyone gained.

DAVID
RUNS A TEMPERATURE

With an ill child you face the problem of helping him settle down for a time to a different kind of life. While he is still sick enough to sleep most of the time, when he takes only a little food and needs mostly rest, quiet, and watching, your problem is comparatively simple. But the time comes when the worst is over and the tedious period of convalescence begins. It's then that you are in for a letdown. As long as your child was really sick, you could rise to the occasion. But now when he's almost well, you may find yourself suddenly tired just as your small patient begins to get restless and demanding. At such times, being prepared for your family's special needs--and your own—is half the battle.

Parents all differ in their skill and pleasure in concocting novelties to amuse the convalescent; some just haven't the knack. If you're one of these, you may find that quite usual routines are just as satisfying. And if your child senses impatience in your manner and learns that a new plaything is merely a prelude to your leaving him alone for long hours, he's likely to resent it. What he wants even more than amusements is a mother who is in and out of his room and who, while she's there, enjoys being with him.

David, as happens to every child now and then, is in for a brief bout with sickness. It's not serious, he'll be well in a week or so. But he has to stay quiet, and this means changes in the usual routines of life, not for him alone, but for the whole family.

All through that afternoon and evening David's mother suspected there was something not quite right about him. He had been cross with everyone and hardly ate any supper. When she heard him call around 2 A.M. she had somehow expected it and went bounding into his room. David says he doesn't feel well and his throat's sore.

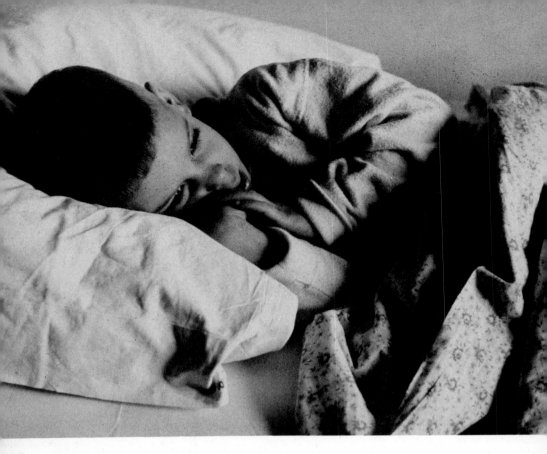

He's restless and his forehead feels hot. Mother gives him half an aspirin tablet, a long drink of water, smoothes his bed out, shakes up his pillow, and sits down awhile, talking quietly about the events of the day.

1

In the morning his head still feels hot and, though he's awake, he's listless and just wants Mother to stay close. Thermometer says 103.2° and she calls the doctor.

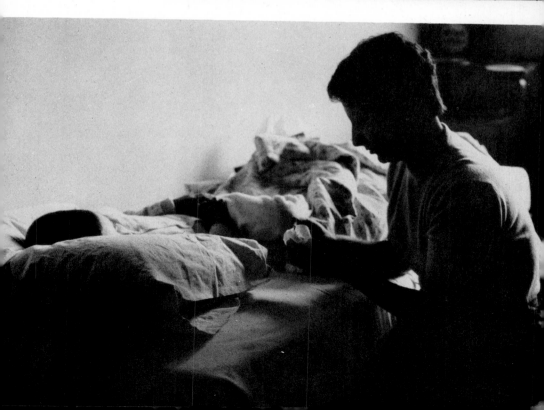

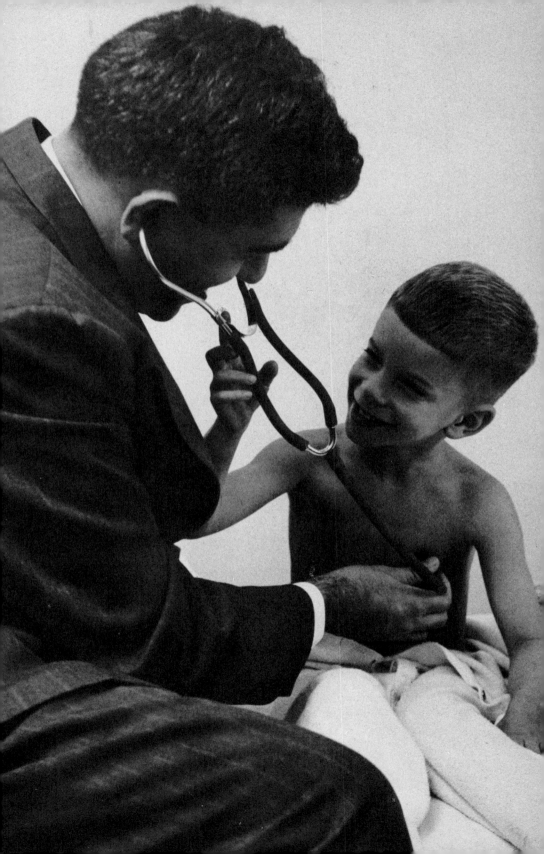

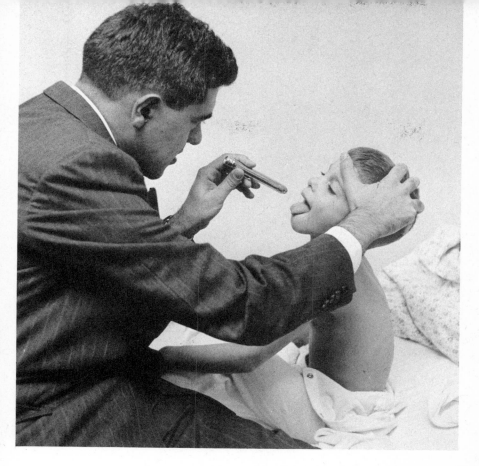

David and the doctor have been great friends ever since David was a baby. David knows all the routines—just how to breathe while the doctor moves the stethoscope around on his chest and back—how to open his throat wide and say "Ah-h-h." Then the doctor writes a prescription and tells David's mother to call and report in the morning.

Mother explains that he won't be able to go to the circus on Saturday because the doctor thinks he'll have to stay home for three or four days. This is bad news; David had been looking forward to the circus for a long time. "Never mind," she says, "it's just postponed. We can return the tickets and get others for later on." David insists he wants to go this Saturday and is pretty cross and angry about it. Mother doesn't argue, soon finds something else to talk about, and the subject doesn't come up again.

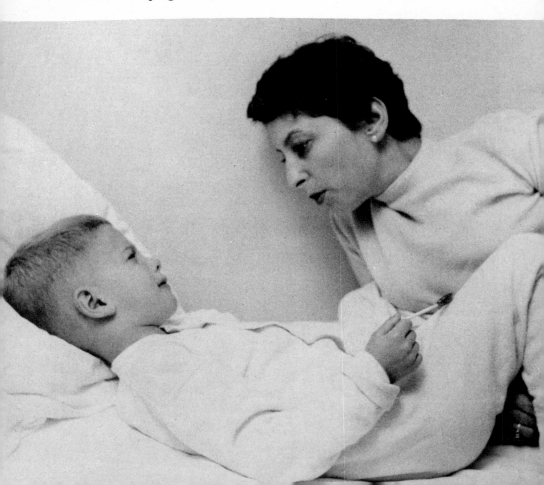

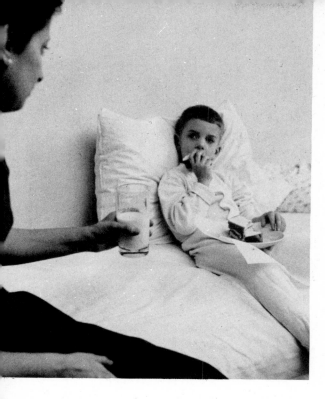

For the next few days David hasn't much appetite and plays for only short periods. He loves having Mother pop into his room often.

Most of the time he's a good patient and takes his medicine as ordered three times a day.

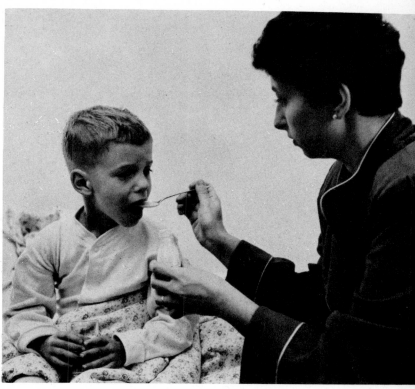

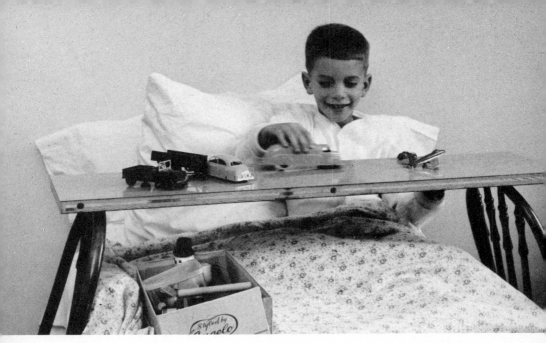

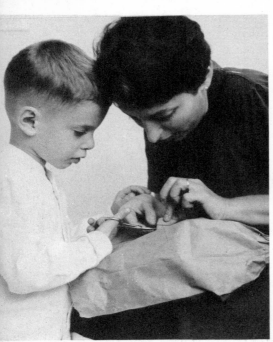

On the second day his temperature has gone down a bit and his throat's not as sore. He has a cough. Now it's harder to keep him busy and happy. The doctor says if he gets too restless in bed he can get up if he's warmly dressed and will play quietly. He and Mother make a mask out of a paper bag from the grocery store.

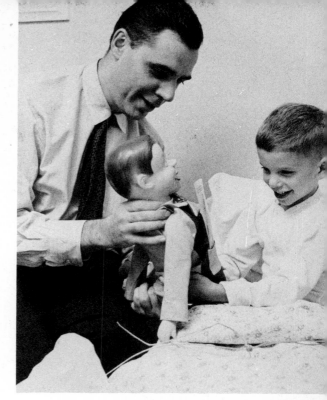

It's Saturday and Dad takes over for the whole day while Mother goes out. It's a great treat to have him all alone for so long. As a surprise, Dad brings Jerry Mahoney—an old TV friend of David's.

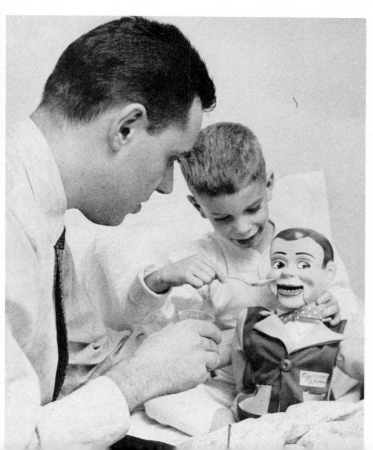

Now come the hardest days of all. David's neither sick nor well. He still isn't allowed to go out, and Mother seems to have a great many things to attend to besides him. He can't find things to do and cries easily. Then Mother realizes he needs her now perhaps more than ever and that she can help him get back to normal.

19

Next day he gets dressed, and from a top closet shelf come a lot of toys David had forgotten existed. His temperature is nearly normal and Mother phones the doctor. "If it's a warm day tomorrow he can go out," he says. "Whoopee," shouts David, bouncing on the bed. He still coughs a bit, looks pale, but will get well fast now. "And I do believe we'll all be going to the circus pretty soon now," says Mother.

The baby-sitter

Twenty-four hours a day of children year in and year out isn't good for either a child or his parents. "Don't tell us that Grandma did it, so why can't we!" they say—and they're right. Grandma had Aunt Sally living nearby, ready and willing to help out. There was Cousin Kate across the street and others, too. In those days families were clans, and they could pinch-hit for each other, minding each others' babies and calling across the fence when they wanted something. Children could be left to play outdoors without fear of traffic or prowlers.

But today, once a baby has arrived, the housebound young parents begin to wonder what's become of the carefree evenings they used to have together, the suppers with friends, the movies, the week ends. For most young couples today, the answer is the sitter. She is a national institution and nobody has to be told so. What you really need to know is how to use this institution successfully and safely.

The responsibility for picking the right kind of sitter is the parents'. Nobody else can really decide with whom it's safe to leave children. In some towns there are regular sitter agencies, and sometimes hospitals or other groups give training courses to would-be sitters, designed to instruct them in infant care or "child psychology." How much good such courses do depends, as with any training, on the individual. In the end the parents must make the choice. There are three main points to consider: Your prospective sitter must be someone who likes children and can get on with them; she must be conscientious enough to carry out your wishes; and she must be levelheaded enough to deal with an emergency. Day-time sitters—who really never get a chance to sit for a second!—need to be chosen even more carefully than those who come for evenings only. They will have more to do with the children in a more varied set of circumstances, and the job calls not only for good sense but for understanding as well. Anyone who has the care of children needs more than the knack of capturing them with a quick superficial appeal. She must be able to meet the dozen and one varied demands which life with young-sters makes, and meet them in ways that at least approximates the parents' standards.

Although this all may sound rather formidable, it is surprising how many women of different ages and circumstances can qualify. Women who have brought up families of their own or schoolgirls who belong to big families often have an easy relationship with children which gets them off to a good start in work of this sort.

Wages vary a good deal with the town and neighborhood. Neigh-bors, schoolteachers, and others who know families and young people probably can tell you about what the current rates are. They are usually higher Saturday nights and after midnight. Daytime sitters should get more than the ones who come after the children are tucked in their beds. A sitter who is asked to do housework other than the children's supper dishes should also be paid extra and there should be a clear understand-ing with her ahead of time as to what is and isn't expected.

She will want to know, too, what's in prospect for her. Whether she's middle-aged or young, the more she gets to be a real friend of the family, the better her relations with the children will be. Knowing something about her family life, taking an interest in her ambitions and plans for herself will help you gauge her capabilities. Whoever she is, she needs a comfortable place to work or read or listen to a tuned-down radio, and the family who has TV is especially sought after. If she's young, she's likely to appreciate generosity about phone calls. Icebox privileges within reason—she shouldn't devour tomorrow's lunch or empty the last bottle of milk—may be extended, especially on evenings when she stays late. If you're delayed in getting home, she should be notified, and at night it is usually the parents' responsibility to see that she gets home safely.

There are certain instructions and other arrangements that must be clearly understood by her. Always leave with her the address and phone number where you may be reached, or, failing that, the number of some other responsible friend or relative. Also be sure she knows how to get in touch with a neighbor and the doctor in case she should need help promptly. If you think there's a chance she might not be able to reach you by phone, make a point of calling her in the course of the evening to make sure all is well.

When all this has been attended to, a well-planned leisurely introduction to the child is basic to good relations. Your youngster at first may show some objections to an unfamiliar sitter. He wants Mother to stay with him and senses that the sitter gives you a chance to escape. The best plan is to have her time and yours overlap a bit and it is well worth the additional cost. Show that you like her and get her to play something with your child and you before you leave her to her chores. Don't go away until everyone's comfortable together and never make the mistake of sneaking off without letting your child know. Even though a firm quiet farewell produces tears and protests, it's better than letting a child suddenly wake to the fact that you've deserted him without taking leave. If you've promised to phone home during the evening, don't let him down, and if you've told him you'll be home by a certain time, do so. Even with the most conscientious handling, a child may cry when the moment for good-by arrives, but if he really likes the sitter he'll usually settle down not long after you've left. Prolonged and intense misery is another matter, and you will want to make it clear to your sitter that if anything like that develops you must be called.

It will make an enormous difference to the family's happiness if you can find someone congenial to help in your home. If you're lucky and watch your chance, you may find a sitter who becomes a real friend, so genuinely interested that she wants to come when you need her, who knows each of your children, and, as she watches them grow older, is almost as proud as you to see each one develop. Women like this offer parents a chance for that much needed freedom to get reacquainted with each other and with themselves. And, like the rest of us, children too gain through a healthy change from their customary routine and the stimulating challenge of a new personality.

WHEN ANN
TAKES OVER

Seventeen-year-old Ann is the eldest of five children, and kids are no news to her. She can't remember the time when there wasn't a young brother or sister clambering over her and wanting something. She was the one who could always stop a quarrel or make any child laugh.

Ann is a senior at the local high school and someday expects to study to be a trained nurse. She's known for her gaiety, is a fine field hockey player and bowler; she loves hillbilly songs. Ann is inclined to be nonchalant about her dates with boys. Some of her girl friends who worry a lot about being popular can't understand how anyone as pretty as Ann can spend a Saturday night every now and then as she does, contentedly stretched on the couch, munching an apple and enjoying the evening paper.

Among the young married couples in her town Ann is in great demand as a baby-sitter. If you're the mother of a family, the biggest favor you can do your friend and neighbor when she runs into a family emergency is to say, "You take Ann. She was to come to me that evening, but you need her more and I'll manage somehow." Needless to say, it's the rare child, too, who, after a few hours with Ann, doesn't jump with joy when he hears she's coming.

It's Ann's first appearance in this home. Sheila's the mamma's girl just now—wants no substitutes.

Mother knew it was going to be hard at first and so arranged for Ann to come two hours ahead of the time she and her husband planned to go out. This would give Sheila plenty of time to get used to Ann. Sheila is gradually won by a pass-the-cracker game. Peter, aged seven, gives advice freely.

Here's what the baby should have for supper. Mother explains, and Lindsay, eleven months, will be more than willing. For both Peter and Lindsay it was love at first sight. A little later Sheila, too, seems willing to stay with Ann while Mother, indoors, gets dressed to go out with her husband.

There are a few last-minute tears from Sheila. Mother explains she'll phone later on. A moment afterward Sheila looks wistfully after the departing car but already is wondering what Ann's promised story will be.

By the end of bath time Sheila has been completely won over. Ann knew such interesting stories it was no trick at all to get Sheila out of the water when the time came.

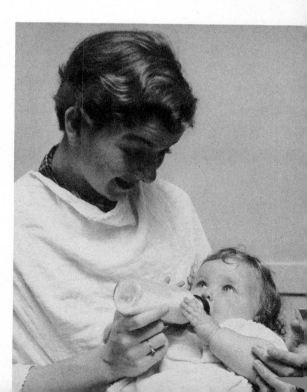

As for Lindsay, her beloved bottle is the answer to everything. Every mother is entitled to one easy child in the batch, thinks Ann.

Sheila's been waiting for one more story. Then, carried off to bed, she is suddenly sound asleep. Ann checks to see that Lindsay is also sleeping peacefully.

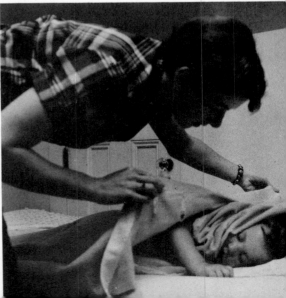

Meanwhile Peter's been waiting patiently to exhibit his skill at his favorite check-ers. He's surprisingly good and beats Ann a few times before she catches on and really starts trying. Peter's a good sport when he loses, and the only trouble is he never wants to stop. Finally Ann has to get him to agree that after two more he'll go off to bed. He may have his light on and read for a while if he wants to.

The noise upstairs was just Peter dropping the checker box. The pieces are rolling all over, but Ann decides to let him cope with it. She needs this time to clear up the children's supper dishes and get their things off the living-room floor. Then she'll have some time to herself and plans to tune in on the "Hit Parade" and look over some magazines.

The telephone rings, and there's Mother to inquire after her brood and especially how Sheila survived the parting. Ann reports that she was a lamb and at this moment sound asleep. "If she wakes, tell her I called," says Mother. "I wouldn't want her to think I forgot. And be sure to help yourself to something in the ice-box if you get hungry," she adds.

Two hours later: Ann makes her report of the evening's events to the returning parents, agrees to come again a week from Thursday.

Hospitals need not be frightening

Lucky is the child who reaches maturity without some hospital experience. Yet with advances in medical diagnosis and the perfecting of techniques in anesthetics and aftercare, we can often forestall future difficulties today with an operation on a small child which would have been unheard of in time past. Probably the operation most commonly performed on children is a tonsillectomy. But because it is comparatively simple for the surgeon and the recuperative period is brief, we are sometimes tempted to dismiss it as a slight and unimportant experience for the child and one that he should be able to meet without fuss or worry.

But even for so minor an operation as this, children need thoughtful and imaginative preparation. Since even for a tonsillectomy doctors now prefer to keep a child in the hospital for twenty-four hours, it's well for parents to consider the possibility and know how to handle it before they're faced with an emergency. If the child has been well prepared, knows what to expect, and if his hospital experience is considerately handled, he will not only make a much better recovery, but he will also be armed against the notion, not at all uncommon with children who have been hospitalized, that he's being abandoned by his parents when he most needs them.

Of course no operation, not even a tonsillectomy, should be undertaken with a small child unless the doctor considers it really necessary. But it is a fact that chronic infection of the tonsils can sometimes threaten a child's hearing, invite germs that cause constant colds, and—with some allergic children—bring on asthmatic attacks. In these cases, it's best if the tonsils come out.

Hospitalization of any kind has disadvantages. Ordinarily the sick child will do better at home in his familiar surroundings if it is at all medically advisable to keep him there. Operations, whenever possible, should be postponed, unless there are sound medical reasons to the contrary, until a child is four or five years old. By then he is better able to grasp what you tell him and understand why he must go to the hospital. This understanding is the best safeguard against the sense of betrayal a child may have when he finds himself suddenly among strangers who do frightening things to him. Above all he needs to know that even if his parents must leave him for a while, they will surely come back. Just because Mother goes away, it doesn't mean she's gone forever. Children often seem to believe that this ordeal which they must face alone and among strangers is somehow punishment for being "bad."

Friendly relations between a child and his doctor make everything easier. A doctor who understands children will explain why the tonsils should come out, what will happen to him when he gets to the hospital, what his room and bed will be like. He needs to know there will be nurses who will take care of him. You or the doctor can tell him he'll be given something to breathe that will put him to sleep and when he wakes his throat may be a bit sore, but the soreness won't last long. He should know just how long his parents will be allowed to stay with him, who will take care of him when they aren't there, and just when they will come back and take him home.

Most doctors know the value of keeping parents—unless they're the nervous kind—as close to young patients as possible, even in hospitals. Visiting hours are getting more flexible and there are provisions in special cases for parents to stay with a child all night. Even if a child cries when his mother leaves, this is far more normal and wholesome than the deadly calm of despair that engulfs the child whose mother seems never to come.

Whenever you can arrange for it, stay close beside your child until he is under the anesthetic or nearly so. A sedative given while he is still in his bed can make him groggy enough so that he'll scarcely notice when he's wheeled off to the operating room without you. If possible, be beside him when he comes to; if you can't, explain just which nurse will be there and just when you yourself will come. Even hospital routines that fall far short of the ideal needn't be too damaging if a child knows what to expect.

Children usually sense it when there's something important in store for them, and parents must reckon on this. A day or two ahead of time is usually soon enough to tell a child of four or five about the coming operation. "Perhaps some day you'll be better off without those tonsils in your throat," you may say. Children often gain self-assurance by "playing tonsillectomy," so encourage your youngster who must go to the hospital to play doctor or mother, with a doll or toy animal as the patient. The doll goes to the hospital, is undressed, and put to bed. Her temperature is taken, she breathes something to put her to sleep after being first assured that Mother will come back when she wakes up. "Your throat will hurt a little bit, darling," a little girl may tell her doll, "but there'll be ice cream and lollipops and presents when you're home again."

With this kind of preparation a child can accept the operation when it comes and be free to enjoy the special attentions that are part of it, emerging at last with pride in a new experience.

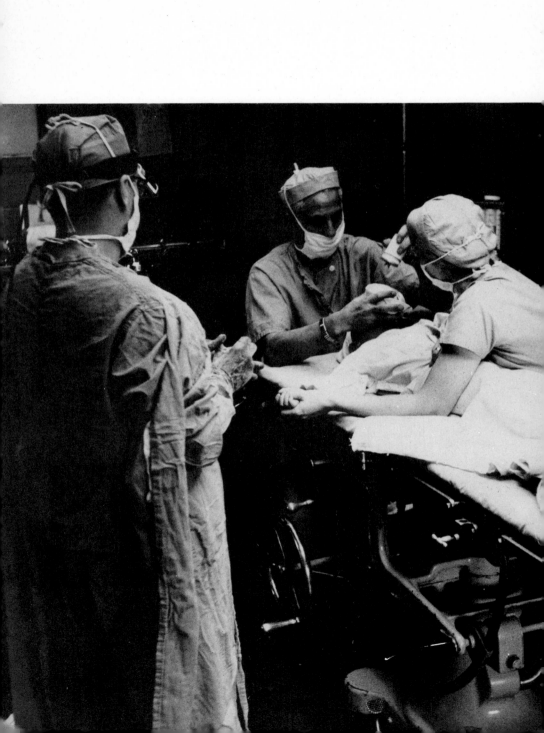

GEORGE
HAS HIS TONSILS OUT

Most doctors today prefer to do even as slight an operation as a tonsillectomy under the most favorable conditions. Though complications are rare, it's a safeguard to be in a hospital where everything's at hand just in case. The surgeon can do this work better if there's an anesthetist to take over that end of the job, and he needs a nurse in the operating room too.

A small child has no way of knowing that all these strange masked figures are really the same kind of nice people he's used to having around him. The unfamiliar surroundings, the weird clothing, the queer smells and shiny instruments are all likely to be terrifying if he is taken by surprise and has to face them alone with only strange people around. That's why doctors have come to feel that a child needs to be prepared for an operation by both his doctor and his parents and that the anesthetic shouldn't be forced on him ruthlessly. Time spent helping a young patient through this ordeal is time well spent, they feel. He recovers faster; his confidence in the fair dealings of grownups remains intact.

Because a child should understand ahead of time just what's going to happen to him when he gets to the hospital, doctors, whenever possible, prefer not to perform an operation until a child is four or five years old, when he can really understand their explanations of why it's necessary and what they're going to do.

Here's how George's doctor and parents helped him meet an ordeal that might have been terrifying but, because of their thoughtful preparation, wasn't.

1

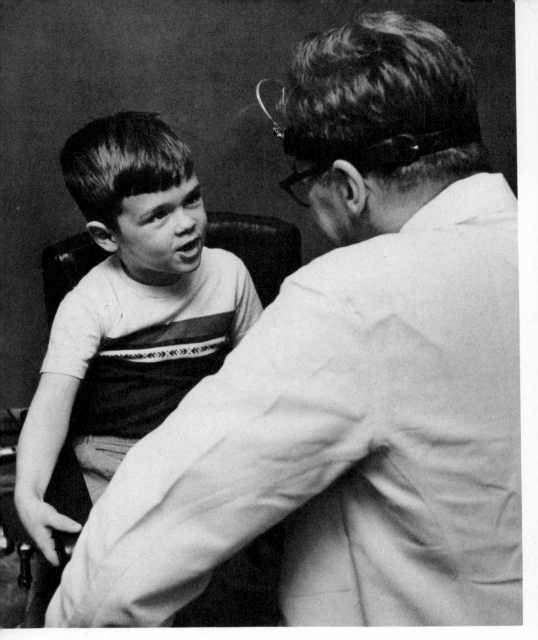

George, aged five, is going to have his tonsils out. Chronic infection and enlargement of the tonsils often lead to impaired hearing, so a tonsillectomy is indicated. He and the doctor are old friends. George knows he can trust him to tell the truth and warn him if something's going to hurt. Now the doctor explains in words George can understand that those tonsils are making him have colds that keep him home in bed a lot when he'd much rather be out playing. Then the doctor lets George ask any questions he wants and answers truthfully. He says he can't promise there'll be no more colds, but he hopes they'll be fewer.

At home Mother explains a few more things. They'll put a mask over George's mouth and nose with something on it to make him go to sleep. She tells him she'll go to the hospital with him and what will happen while he's there. She knows that each hospital does things a little differently and she has questioned the doctor to know just how things will be handled in George's case. Later George plays operation with his toy dog.

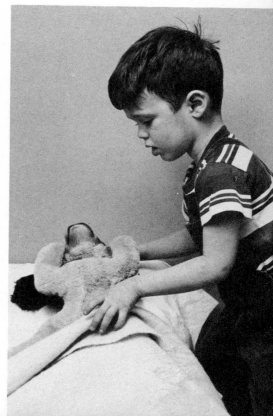

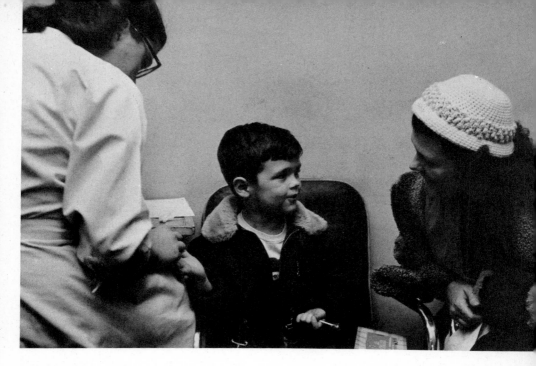

In spite of everything, George is a bit scared when he's finally off to the hospital. Poochy's a help.

Here's one of the nurses Mother told him about, and she gives him a lollipop and tells him she's going to take a drop of blood from his finger. "It may hurt just a tiny bit," the nurse says.

Time to go to his room, and George is suddenly scared. Mother just pats him a bit, doesn't say much. Soon he's ready.

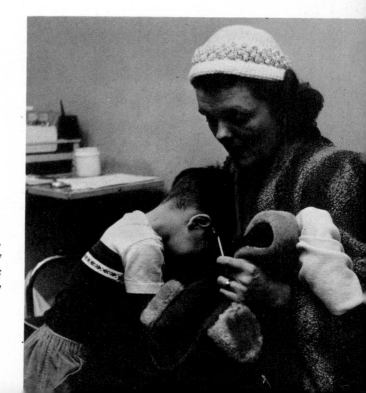

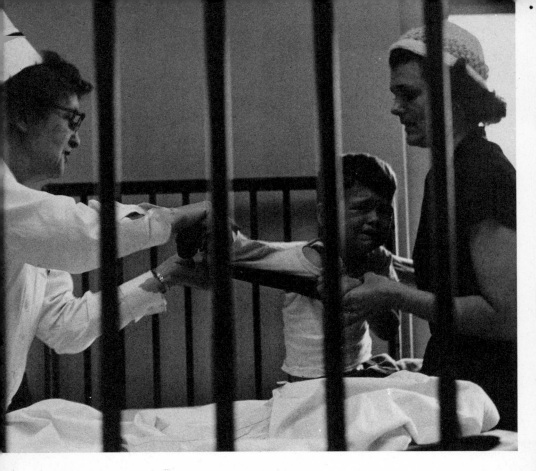

Upstairs there's another nurse, who helps Mother get George to bed. The nurse thinks he ought to hurry, and that gets George a little excited and he whimpers and complains. But when he's all ready the nurse is very nice after all and brings out a lot of picture books he's never seen before. As soon as Mother realizes that George is happy with a friendly nurse, she stays in the background and just puts in a word now and then. A new doctor comes to take his blood pressure, and finally he gets a sedative. Now he's a drowsy little boy and Mother reads to him.

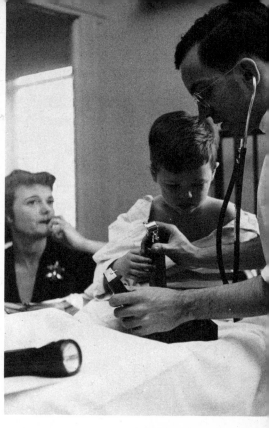

In the operating room he sits up. Mother is gone now. But the people are just the way she said they'd be. They're dressed all in green and wear masks, but above the masks he sees nice eyes twinkling. The doctor lets him play with his operating headlight.

2

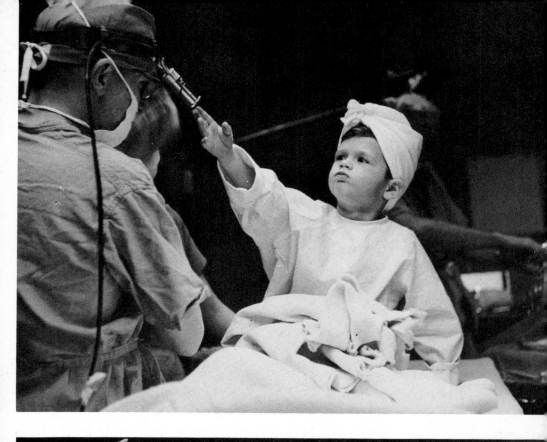

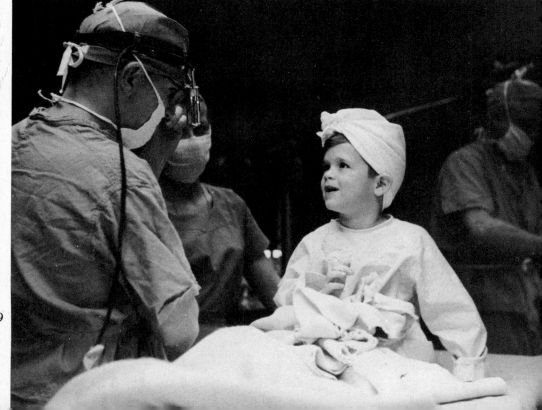

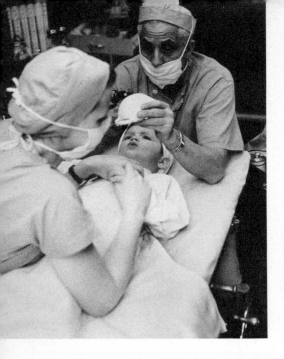

"Now I'm going to give you something to breathe," the doctor says after a while. "It won't hurt, but if you don't like it, just take a long breath and blow it away." George remembers just how hard he blew when he blew out his birthday candles—and he takes a big breath. Outside, his nurse and Poochy are waiting for him.

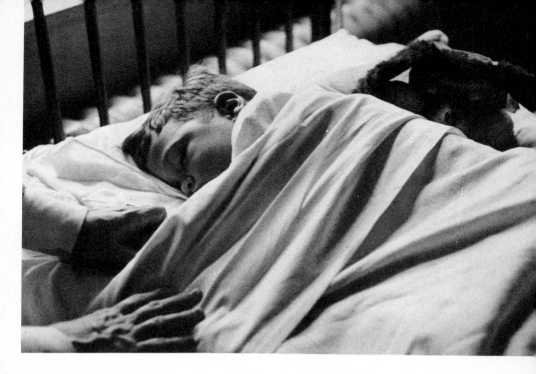

True to her word, Mother's voice is the first one George hears as, only half conscious, he complains of a sore throat. "Tonsils are all out, Georgie," Mother says. "You were wonderful."

Next morning George is feeling pretty fit, but his throat's still sore. He'll be given aspirin. And here's Dad to admire a tonsilless throat. "And they tell me you were very brave, Georgie," he says.

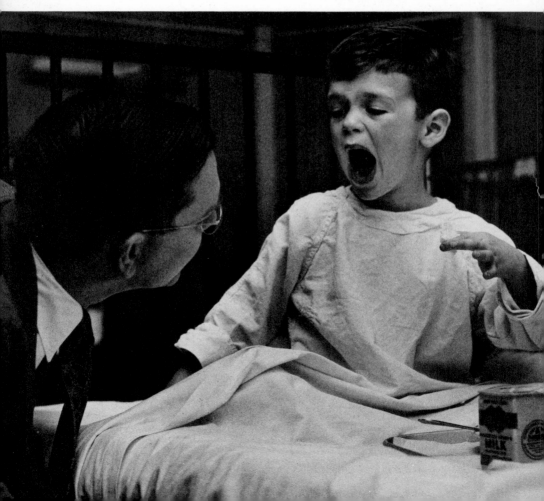

A few days later George is as good as ever. "See my throat," he calls to some admiring friends. "Didn't hurt a bit!" Through the window they take a good look.

The world of play and friends

When he's still quite a baby, your child will begin to show interest not only in toys and "things" in his world, but in other children too. He stares hard at them, perhaps. Or he makes a grab for the other child. He may even cry when the visitor goes away. All through the second year of life the fascination grows, although at times there may be a touch of anxiety in it too; the young child doesn't yet know quite how to get along with this other human, who is so important yet doesn't act a bit like a grownup.

When they're around three years old, most children really begin to get the hang of what playing with others means. They begin to learn the difference between mine and thine, to wait their turn, to share their plans and belongings with another. The idea that others have rights is beginning to take root, and so is the thought that affection and approval may be even more worth having than possessions. They are now on the way to learning the lessons of give-and-take, and their relations to other youngsters grow steadily more absorbing. Nursery school, if there is a good one in the neighborhood, offers these opportunities under wise supervision and may be a deeply satisfying experience. But throughout these years before school begins, and sometimes afterward, children will need lots of help from you still. Selfish, grabby ones need your help in learning to hold back. Timid, passive ones need some protection, but can respond amazingly to encouragement to go ahead and stand up for themselves when the help comes from someone who is really resourceful and doesn't merely nag.

All this takes a lot of time, and you may be tempted to make the all too frequent mistake of trying to hurry your child on this long road to becoming a social being. The two-year-old who "just loves other children" may still be better off if he has them in restricted doses. Three- to

5

five-year-olds will need your pretty constant presence and patient skillful guidance. Even older ones, as we all know, need grownups around and some direction now and then. There are no two alike, either. Children differ widely in the age and speed with which they learn an easy give-and-take and most parents have been oversold on the value of early and continuous play with other children. We tend to forget that our youngsters need grownups in their lives, too, as friends and as intimates. They should also have plenty of quiet play alone or just time to loaf now and then when they feel like it.

But from about three years old on, most children are on the way to making some place for themselves among others of their age, whether it's in the back yard, on the sidewalk in front of your house, in the playground, or in nursery school. They can profit not only from being with other children, but from having friends among grownups and by a gradually widening scene which includes people of many kinds outside the family. Now is the time they begin to be insatiable for things to play with and through play to learn the skills they will need throughout life. With these skills comes a growing sense of mastery over the tangible world around them. For children, play is everywhere. It's in toys, of course. But more often it's in the kitchen cupboard, in Mother's dressing table, in the puppy next door, in the planks over the gutter, in the dump heap in the back lot, in precious collections of miscellaneous junk.

Play is learning to feel, too. The same small boy with cowboy suit and gun, who discovers, one minute, what it's like to be big and powerful, next minute is developing feelings of protective tenderness as he cuddles his kitten. His small sister is already in rehearsal for motherhood as she dresses her dolls or tucks them into bed.

Through their play, children find for themselves a stage on which they can discharge all those unruly emotions which can cause so much trouble when bottled up inside. It does them good to use color in strange "designs" all over a sheet of paper—more good than trying to paint accurate portrayals of objects. And they need scope to climb and shout and whoop it up in homemade dramas. Later, through sports and games, they will have further outlets to channel those aggressive feelings that are so deeply a part of all of us. Their need to dominate others will become bound by rules of the game and by standards of sportsmanship.

Sometimes your children's play will be eager and active. At other times there may be periods of withdrawal and inaction which trouble you vaguely but which may also tempt you to accept the situation too complacently. "It's a phase," you say hopefully. "He'll grow out of it." This isn't enough. Though the shyer, more withdrawn child may be busy growing inwardly in ways that are all his own, there's also a possibility that he may have bogged down and now needs someone to set him going again. "Which is it?" you wonder. It's not easy to be sure or to know for certain what you should do. No one can tell you exactly, but if you watch carefully, your knowledge of your child and his own special problems will be your surest guide.

MAUREEN
IS ALWAYS BUSY

Where there are a lot of children in the family, as with five-year-old Maureen, what to do is never a problem. There's always someone to play with and belongings accumulate. Maureen's home has a yard with space and play equipment that draw neighbors' children. The sidewalk out front offers additional space to ride a bike, skate, play hopscotch. A large family has its troubles too. When brothers and sisters play together, they also fight. There are tensions among them that may produce a crisis every hour. Of the neighbors' children, some are all you could wish for, others aren't at all what you'd wish for. There are the eternal cliques, where your child either "belongs" or where they won't let him play. This is the stuff of life that every child—with help from parents—must learn to cope with.

Sometimes Maureen, like everyone, needs to get away from it all and just be a person all by herself. This solitude, too, is necessary for a child's growth. Whether she's being a little mother wholly concentrated on the needs of her child or whooping it up as an Indian warrior, Maureen feels strongly, lives intensely.

"Helping" their parents is one of the important ways by which children slowly gain a sense of responsibility, for they learn that there are things everyone has to do—even a grownup. Maureen knows her parents won't be satisfied till all the leaves are raked up and burned, and she helps for all of ten minutes—not bad for a five-year-old.

2

Learning to catch is a part of basic equipment for children. They differ greatly in their innate capacity for co-ordination. Realizing this, parents should try to give less skillful children some practice alone. If exposed prematurely to the superior performance of their friends, they may be paralyzed by discouragement.

Toys and sports are only a small part of play. There's endless excitement in the world at one's doorstep.

Maureen and her friends have discovered the joys of the gurgling water beneath the grating of the sewer, are entranced by watching sticks and papers they toss into it get whirled away into the unknown.

1

Pets have enormous meaning for children and evoke a whole range of emotion—
joy at their funny antics, sorrow when they're lost or die, tenderness because
they're weak and need protection. Pets often make children aware, too, of their
own cruel impulses. They're ashamed of them and may need understanding help
from parents in learning to transform them.

Though children should be expected to take some responsibility for their
pets, its rare that they can take sole responsibility. Parents should be prepared to
help; their own concern for the animal is the most important factor in the child's
learning to feel the same way.

The meal over, Maureen starts yanking on her puppy's leash quite a bit harder than she needs to. Then, frightened and guilty at her own impulses, she stoops to comfort the ever-forgiving canine.

A daily frustration: Maureen can't give up the hope that her big brother and his friends are going to let her play with them, but they don't. Concealing her feelings for the moment, she lets them out a while later on little brother.

The family record player has something for all ages. There's classical music, folk songs, dance music, and jazz. The children pick up words and tunes galore—and they dance in impromptu fashion, too, as the spirit moves them.

85

It's a fine thing to be all alone with brush and colors, making wonderful "pictures" on big pieces of paper. Nobody says "What's that?" Maureen wouldn't know, feels only deep joy in the doing.

The perennial pleasures of "dress up" are greater whenever Maureen's big brother—his friends aren't around—condescends to play too.

Just Maureen and Mother! And once again there's the fun of helping with real work. They tell stories, sing songs together, or just chat as they work. Maureen feels very happy. Mother knows that unless she can be alone now and then with each one of her brood she loses track of what's going on inside of them. Deeply satisfying to her is the child's eager response to these moments of intimacy, so easy to lose in a large family where household chores are never done.

7

TV and utter absorption! Is it good for them? Mother and Father wonder. Like the automobile, they decide, TV has come to stay but needs regulation. With suggestions from all, the family agrees to forgo poor programs, adopts a workable schedule for the good ones.

When Dad suggests a game of slapjack, even TV can wait. After Maureen has played a game or so, the baby gets his turn but just slaps anything. And later— the great and wonderful world of books begins here in this happiest hour of the day.

The child who is shy

What can you do for your child who is shy and has trouble joining quickly and happily with others at play? Brigades of parents and teachers have puzzled their heads over what to do for these more timid children who tend to hang back and in the end the grownups come to realize that slow sympathetic help is what wins the day.

First what *not* to do:

Don't force your child to go places or do things that are going to make him miserable.

Don't comment on his shyness in front of others. ("What's the matter? Have you lost your tongue?" or even, "Oh dear, he's so terribly shy!")

Don't laugh at him or try to kid him out of a fault that's more painful for him than for you. Don't try, either, to pretend it doesn't matter.

The shy child may merely be one who is a little slower than others in feeling at home in a group; he isn't necessarily headed for abnormality or unpopularity. Shyness doesn't mean he's going to be a sissy or even that he will never be a leader. In his own time the chances are that, with some help, he'll come out of his shyness and find a place for himself among others.

Let him play for a while quietly and in his own way. Help him develop skills and interests of all kinds. Show him you enjoy his company. Show him too that you enjoy other people, both grownups and children, and watch your chance to draw him into your conversation with them or whatever it is you're doing. Make your home a place where children like to come and take trouble to make them comfortable and happy in it.

When your shy child is out of his home among strange, perhaps rougher children, you may have to maneuver so that the first steps toward mixing aren't too hard for him. Gentle children or younger ones perhaps may be less frightening companions than big bumptious ones and give a shy youngster time to build up greater ease and self-confidence. But in taking steps to protect a child from the kind who may be too much for him, be careful you don't *over*protect. The day will come when his strength may be greater than you realize.

If you find there's just one other child with whom yours likes to play, encourage the friendship. Don't belittle it or try to force your child prematurely into being a good mixer. For some children a "best friend" is a very important and deep experience, valuable in itself and, when a child is inwardly ready, a steppingstone to an expanded world.

DAVID
MAKES A FRIEND

David was one of those shy, wistful children to whom the heart of all grownups just naturally went out. They wanted to help this quiet, "different" child find a happy place for himself among other youngsters. They wanted to draw him in when there were games and fun going on. But David was slow to respond. Mostly, he just hung around on the edges of things with big sad eyes. His father and mother, like many other parents, hoped that this was only a passing phase. Sometimes they insisted that he take his chance with the gang. Oftener they just let him alone to play quietly by himself. Then one summer fate intervened. A competent little girl took him in hand for reasons unknown and, through her magic, helped David make big strides forward. David's parents looked and marveled, remained for a while in the background, held their breath—and finally realized how they best could help.

The other children are up in a tree playing Tarzan. David wishes he could too, but doesn't know how to begin. Later, though the lamb draws him, the children still frighten him.

Picture books are his everlasting solace. In the world of make-believe he can imagine he's a powerful hero and forgets all his troubles. His parents realize that he needs books while he still hasn't learned to be active in other ways, but they will be very happy when David no longer has to use them as an escape from his unsolved problems. David senses how they feel but doesn't know what else to do.

Along comes Alexandra. David has been watching her from a great distance for several weeks but never dreamed she'd ever notice him. But now she sits down near him, has a great deal to say, and finally gives David a kiss. "I want you for my friend," she says very definitely, "I like you better than anybody, David."

Before long David's parents realize that Alex is a new force in David's life, and there's danger of his being a helpless victim of her charms. They aren't quite sure what Alex is up to and they feel a little uneasy. What's it all about? they wonder. They're happy that David has a friend, but they want him to develop actively and independently—not merely as Alex's shadow or a tool for anything she may take it into her head to do.

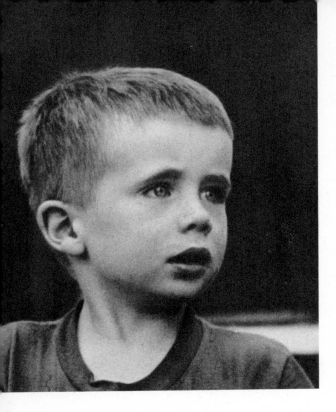

There are lots of exciting playthings in David's house, and Father and Mother urge Alex to come often. Alex takes over with clay and modeling tools and goes right to work insisting that David should too. She shows him how and he pays very close attention.

For a while he just enjoys messing around and showing off his fingers all stuck up with clay. But after a while he begins to make things. There are long moments when he's even more interested in what he's making than in Alex.

Alex has told David that she knows a secret place in the woods. "Let's go," says David suddenly. They're off. For the first time he leads, she follows.

The secret hide-out is an abandoned shed a few yards back in the woods. The two children climb around on it and David is much braver than he's ever been before. He thinks it's the very happiest day of his whole life.

1

Alex administers first aid to a wounded hero. This is lots better than being a space man!

By the end of the summer David's still devoted to Alex, but it's no longer the only thing in his life. Gradually, as his self-esteem grew through friendship with Alex, he's been able to play more and more with other children. "Bet David's afraid of the water," one of them says when they're all in the pool one day. "Betcha I'm not," retorts David, and flops down with all the others.

Jealousy

"If you let Ellie do it, why can't I? Why can *she* get away with just anything?" "I don't want to stay here with Bea; I hate her. I want to go with Bob and Joe!" "Huh, girls! They get all the handouts around this house!" We've all heard these or similar wails, and often they are only a very vocal expression of a passing mood or an honest opinion that grownups might express more temperately. Most children learn to accept their brothers and sisters as familiar, even agreeable parts of the scenery—and finally with affection. But with others it's not so easy. For these the very same words may actually be only a mild hint of the searing emotion that inspired them. A younger child may hotly contest the privileges of an elder; a girl may nourish deep resentments because she wants to be a boy and be accepted by her brothers; a boy may resent the favors he imagines his older sister receives because she is a girl. A child may bitterly resent the arrival of a new baby. When it comes to jealousy, almost anything can happen, for jealousy is a devastating emotion and it can be just as painful for a child as for a grownup.

Yet these sudden storms of anger, brought on perhaps by a trivial incident, often alternate with moments of real pride and protectiveness toward the rival and sudden bursts of affection that are quite bewildering. When love and hate thus go hand in hand, a child is bound to be at war with himself, and sorely needs his parents' steadfast help. But how can they best give this help?

Perhaps the first step is for parents to learn to accept their children as they are and appreciate each for what he has to offer. No two children can ever be alike, and some are easier to get on with than others; though you may love them all, you like them differently. So accept the challenge and work steadily for a better relationship with your more difficult child. It may be that he only needs to air his gripes fully and without fear of moral lectures. He may need new incentives to develop special skills which win for him your appreciation and his own self-respect. He may need people and activities outside the family circle. Freed for a while from the irritations he endures at home, he gains confidence and strength. In this way both he and his parents are relieved from the tensions that have been piling up, and both are better able to make a fresh start.

Because parents nowadays are so aware that favoritism may be one of the cardinal crimes of parenthood, they tend to fall over backwards trying to avoid it. But let's admit it—there will be shades of difference in how we feel. How can you help smiling at Debbie, who tucks her head so confidingly under your chin, while Kenny goes cold at any show of affection and is forever doing things that make you ashamed before your friends? And why does Mary go right on thinking you like Sue better, when you've done everything under the sun to see that Mary gets her share? She harbors grudges no matter what you do.

And then, perhaps, you find yourself beginning to overpraise and actually favor the difficult jealous child at the expense of the other. Or, when the new baby is born, you spend all your time and attention on your first child and don't dare go near the bassinet except when he's out of the house. This usually only makes matters worse, for, if a child begins to suspect that he can really control his mother and keep her away from her other children, he grows only more confused. Dimly he knows that his own safety depends on the strength of his parents and if he finds them playing favorites his confidence in them is shaken. Besides, a child needs to see his mother give the new baby the tender care an infant obviously needs. If she doesn't give it, he is bound to wonder whether she neglected him too, when he was a baby. If so, might she fail him again?

To a child, a "good" mother is one who cares for all her children. In the long run he feels safest with parents who make it clear that each one of their children is precious. Though times may come when one or another may get special consideration, none of them need have any doubts that he gets his share of help in his hour of need, his quota of praise when he earns it.

Little by little as he sees that his mother and father are fair, that they give generously of their time and sympathy, even a jealous child learns to accept a rival. Yearning to grow up and be like his parents, he follows when they set the pace, acts as they act, learns finally to feel as they feel. Against this background, he discovers that in spite of his jealousy and

misdeeds he can depend on you and that, mysteriously enough, you continue to accept him for what he is. He learns at last that even jealousies are not fatal and that, in the long run, the whole family belongs together.

HARD MOMENTS
WITH A RIVAL

No matter how thoughtfully parents prepare a child for a new member of the family or how steadfastly they later show him their love and continuing interest, there will always be some who feel their world threatened to its foundations by a newcomer.

Adam, aged five when baby Peter arrived, showed his jealousy in every muscle of his face and hands. What made it hard was that he half loved Peter too. Peter was *his* little brother; he had been telling his friends for a long time that Peter was on the way and he was proud when they came and admired him. Why couldn't he feel proud all the time instead of wanting so often just to hurt the baby and be rid of him? What made it even harder was knowing that Mother really wanted him to love Peter and that even though she went on smiling at him she was sorry about his jealousy. With these warring emotions, Adam had a hard time for a while.

But somehow, as time went on, things got better. Adam got used to the baby; someday—just as Mother said—he would learn to love him too.

Sometimes children show their tension by all sorts of clowning.

25

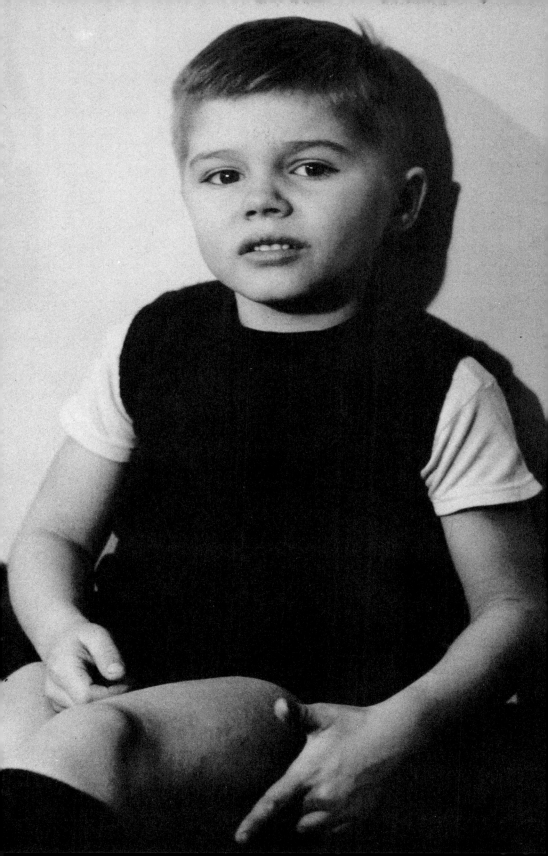

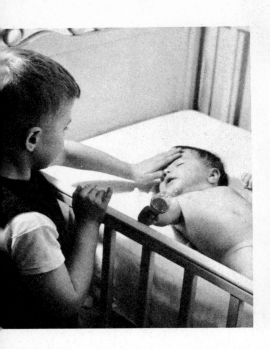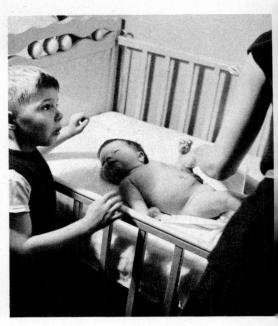

Adam is alone with the baby while Mother is busy in the next room. Peter looks very cunning and soft and helpless, and Adam feels tender toward him and wants to love and fondle him as Mother does. He reaches out a hand to pat him and suddenly has an overwhelming impulse to push his face very hard and angrily.

Just then Mother comes back. Adam pulls his hand away quickly. Mother smiles at him, but he's sure she knows just how bad the thoughts were that were going on inside him. She must know, too, how near he came to hurting Peter. "Did you take good care of our baby?" Mother asks, and adds, "We must be gentle and not hurt him or he might go away and never come back."

Her words were well meant, but they frighten Adam. If that happened it would certainly be his fault. Then surely his parents could never love him again and he would be all alone and unprotected. He looks at the bars of the baby's crib and remembers he has heard that bad people are put behind bars. He crawls under the bed. Then he announces, "I'm in jail now."

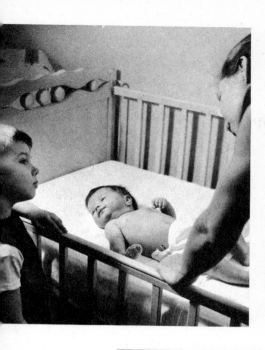
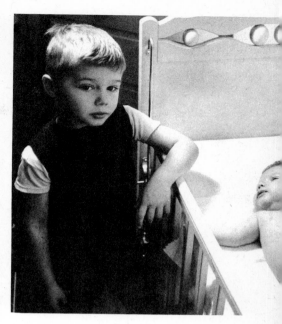
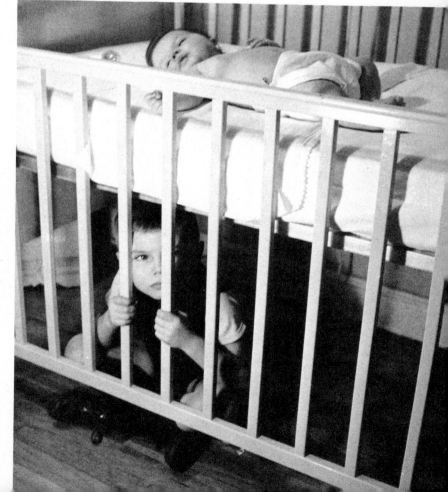

But jail was lonely and he peeks out to see what's happening.

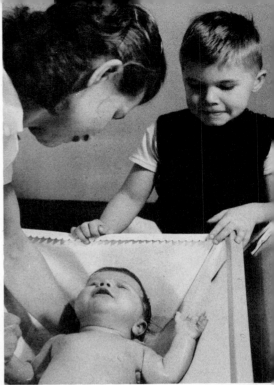

Watching Mother care for Peter is very hard for Adam to take.

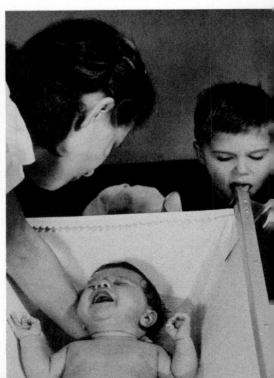

In this distress he gnaws the end of the tub unhappily.

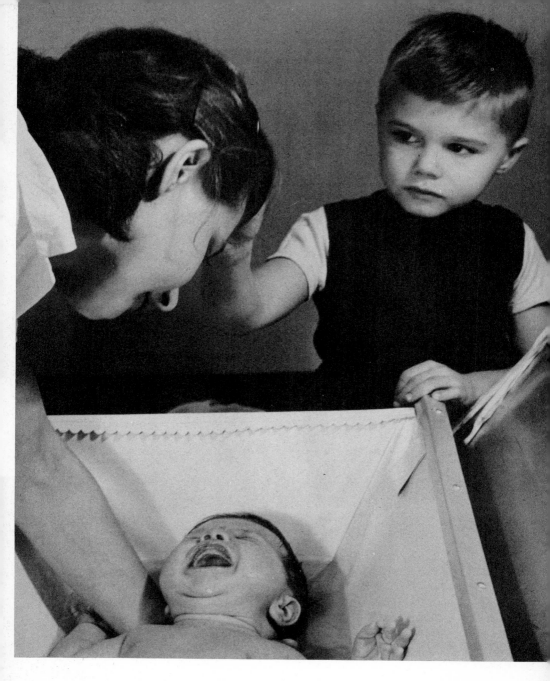

Peter is screaming now, and yet Mother goes right on smiling and talking softly to him. Adams wants Mother to smile only at him, to talk only to him. He doesn't know how to say all the things he's feeling, so he just touches her hair, hoping she'll leave Peter and pay attention to him again.

1

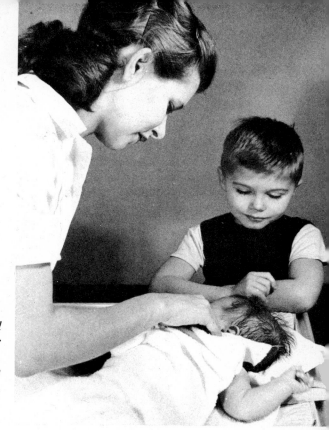

All the while she's drying and dressing Peter he tries to get her attention. Finally a book does it. She stops for a minute and looks at the picture Peter shows her, then tells him she must finish feeding the baby.

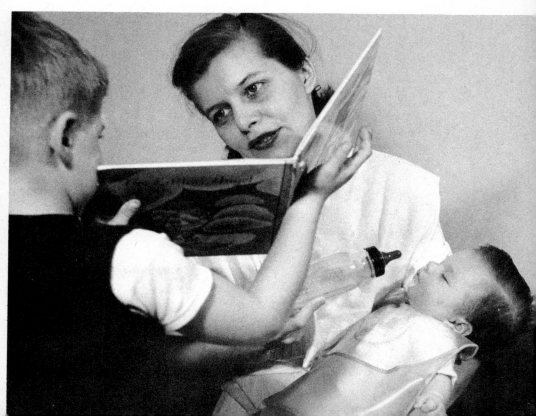

Now Peter's been put away in his crib at last and Adam has Mother to himself. He acts very wild for a time but finally agrees to settle down beside her quietly.

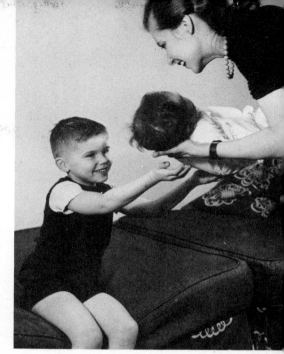

But little by little things get better
for Adam. He learns to trust both
Mother and himself. More and more
now when Mother puts Peter into
his arms he is won by the baby's
funny faces. But it all takes time.

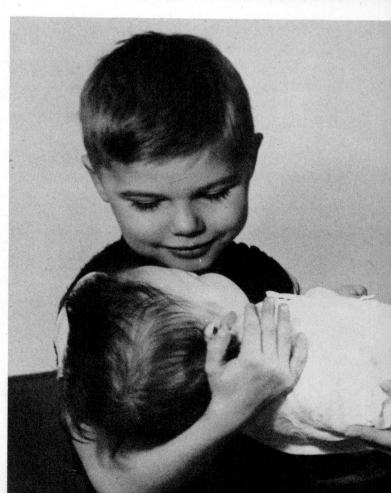

Deeper values
for the family

As your children get older you will probably find yourself giving more and more thought to how you can pass on to them those enduring values that most of us call religious or spiritual values. You know something wonderful is happening when your child begins to be sensitive to all the beauty and mystery of the world around him. You want to encourage this and help him to ask deep questions and philosophize. You realize, too, that you owe him something that goes deeper than all the material advantages you might give—you owe him those inner moral guides that are based on our faith that every human being, no matter how humble, has worth and a kind of sacredness.

How do children come by these values? What can you, their parents, do to pass them on? The small child, we know, is fundamentally self-centered and only gradually learns that others have rights equal to his. But little by little he does discover the satisfactions that come with giving as well as getting. Later, as he matures, he finds that life is enriched by sympathy for other people in his small world and everywhere. He absorbs these values as he absorbs everything else—first and foremost from his parents and through the discovery of what it is they live by.

Very early, children find that their parents set special store by truth, by fair play, and by kindness. Though you are patient with their selfishness and fits of anger, you quietly lead the way toward something different and better. They discover without having to be told that you are happy in doing an act of kindness to a friend. A little later they may notice that it isn't only the agreeable neighbor next door. You are concerned too about the unimportant stranger, who is "different" perhaps, and whose gratitude yields no tangible returns. The time comes when children make the important discovery that their parents will often go to a lot of trouble and take a lot of time to stand up for fair play and justice, not only for their own friends and family but even for people who may be "unpopular" in their own circle. If they find you capable of feeling strongly about ideas, too—so strongly that you are willing to bother to do something about them—these attitudes and this way of life in parents will never pass your children by; these are what determine the values they will live by.

Some people depend on inner sources of strength and on the wisdom of great men of all times and places to guide them through life. But over the centuries most have turned to the church of their ancestors to help them in this quest for strength and wisdom. Churches, on their side, ask you as parents to do your share in passing our common faiths on to our children, well aware that they are handicapped if they must perform this task entirely alone. You too are likely to find that you cannot turn a child over to any institution and expect it to teach him ideals to which you yourselves are lukewarm. Your own innermost convictions—or lack of them—weigh too heavily in the balance. Churches can reinforce and clarify, they can offer opportunities for service, they can help you discover new meanings in religious practices. They can infuse poetry and beauty, bring depth and authority to bear from the storehouse of the past. But every step of the way, churches need as partners, parents who in their homes acknowledge the same goals, share their vision, and care enough to try to translate ideals into action.

Like parents, churches and their ministers vary in the clearness of their thought, the skill by which they communicate their faith to others, their courage in assuming moral leadership. But throughout the nation there is new life stirring. In thousands of communities, a church is often the only voice which speaks for the spirit—which asks people to think deeply and act courageously, to have some clear plan for the deeper life of themselves and their children, and to make decisions which go to the very roots of living.

DEBBY
GOES TO CHURCH

Here's Debbie, happy in her Sunday best, but even happier because in this sanctuary, with her hand in Mother's, she's beginning to feel part of something bigger than herself, bigger even than the grownup men and women around her.

Jim and Elfrieda Lilly, her parents, want their children to grow up in the kind of church that takes seriously the doctrine of the brotherhood of man—and works for it. They agree they have found it in the First Congregational Church in their home town of Akron, Ohio. Here the minister, with the support of the parish, believes·that a church must find ways to draw all its members into a community dedicated to ever-deepening thought and widening sympathies.

As members of this church, the Lillys are working to give practical help to people of all kinds in the neighborhood and city. They attend study groups and forums where they learn more about complex social problems, including peace among nations. They become acquainted, too, with some of the thought and ideals of leaders of other religions. In work and recreation, as well as at worship, rich and poor, old and young, colored and white are equally welcome.

In all its planning, this church emphasizes the family. Children and grownups all do their parts—separately sometimes, together oftener. Rarely is a child "sent" to Sunday school by parents who hold aloof. They believe that if religious faith is to enter into the lives of children, it must be equally a part of family life, honored at home as well as in church.

In homes like the Lillys', where parents give time and thought to the expression of deep convictions, Debbie and the other two children can hardly fail to grasp their message.

*At breakfast this Sunday morning Debbie sits between her father and sister Win-
nie. They pause, as they always do before meals, for a moment of quiet and
thankfulness. A little before nine o'clock they all start off for church. Each has
important matters to attend to before church services at eleven o'clock. That's
brother Jimmy beside Dad.*

2

Church is something like home. You know all the things around you because you've seen them so often. You know nearly all the people. At the early half-hour children's service attended by parents, too, Debbie seems to be not quite sure how to find the hymns.

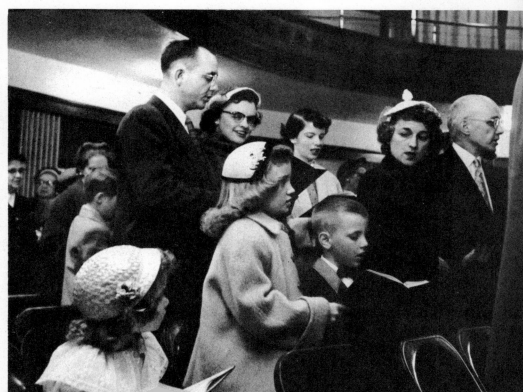

Afterward children scatter to their various activities, watched over by parents who take turns. Debbie dons a smock and attacks her painting wholeheartedly.

At the same time, sister Winnie goes to her choral group led by a choir master. She is becoming familiar with old church music, including Bach.

One of the fathers supervises Jimmy's group for games and stories, and Debbie's mother takes charge of the Babes in Arms while her father is at the church door to welcome the families as they enter.

3

Time to go home and Debbie, her smock put away, takes one last go down the slide. Time has passed quickly, but there's Sunday dinner waiting at home.

Before leaving, the family stops for a chat with the minister. They discuss plans for the woman's club. The program next year will include meetings with prominent speakers from the university but with everyone participating. They will also put on a "musical." Debbie and the other youngsters keep putting in their two cents' worth. Sunday's the happiest day in the week.

The great new adventure

Starting school marks dramatically the boundary between nursery dependence and the new life that comes to a child when he enters the wide world alone. Every child senses this and, behind his resolute front, has inward qualms. Every parent, too, along with his glow of pride, feels his throat tighten as he watches the small son or daughter step gallantly across the threshold to be swallowed up in the big building. But the break can be enormously eased for everyone if the child has already developed the emotional readiness needed to be away from home and "on his own." How can his parents help him find it?

Readiness for school has little to do with advance skills in the three Rs. There's no real gain for a child in having the jump on his fellows: he'll be better off taking his place on a par with the rest and following with them the path to learning. But during the first few days he shouldn't be so unprepared that he feels uncomfortable in a strange place among strange people. There are many ways to arm him in advance. You may arrange for him to know one or two children in his grade ahead of time. Perhaps there's an older friend or brother who has been at school before him who can take him around and give him confidence. A teacher whose name and face are familiar, a building where the long corridors have been visited before—all these will help him feel at home. But, even lacking these, if his life up to now has offered a range of experiences where he's learned to build self-confidence and acquired zest for new experiences, school is likely to come as yet another adventure—and the best adventure of all.

During these preschool years from three to five, a child with sensible parents will have been encouraged to step out gradually from the four walls of his home, and will have had a chance to explore his surroundings. The country child can know animals and see food growing in the fields, loaded onto trucks for market, or brought in to his own dinner table. He should have a chance to hang around farm machinery and watch how his father keeps it in order. With help he may learn what the various seasons bring and how to get ready for them. His world widens when he goes to town where everything is crowded and different.

With a town child the process is reversed. The traffic on the streets is an early all-important fact of his life. Parents should explain about the change of lights at crossings, teach him to recognize the policeman on the corner and get to know him as a friend. Living in a maze of streets and houses, he needs to know his own address and telephone number, his own and his parents' name, so that his sense of identity in the crowded world is secured. Guided by a grownup he can explore shops and their contents—learn what buying and selling means, to recognize coins, and how to handle money for small purchases. With his father, he may visit railroad tracks and sidings, ride on buses, trains, autos, or boats. He can make trips to the country, too, where everything is spread out and green.

Whatever widens a child's range of experience and opens his eyes to the things around him will help him later with school and learning. The people who come into his life prepare him for school too. Getting along with children his own age turns out to be quite different from life with parents or other grownups. He has to take his chances among them and discover what fair play means. So, in preparation for this, long before school days arrive, he will have begun the difficult lessons of sharing, of waiting one's turn, of being a good loser, of not being a crybaby, so that by the time he gets to school he'll know what to expect.

Nursery school or kindergarten—if there's a good one at hand— often helps prepare a youngster for real school. Here the child who is ready to leave the shelter of home and Mother for a few hours a day, learns that he's safe among other children and other grownups. Here's stimulus, too, for creative play and creative relationships of all kinds. Well timed, life in nursery school often affords relief from the tensions that pile up in family life during these years before school begins. But how a child feels about going is very important. If he senses that he's being sent away so Mother can be alone with the new baby, or because she can't manage his tempers, or because she just wants to be rid of him, he may well resent the whole idea. A child of three or four is likely to need help in making the transition to the larger more impersonal world of nursery school. When he first goes, his mother had better plan to stay for the whole morning at first, then perhaps for a part of the time, until gradually the child feels secure and is really willing to be left.

At five, four, or even a younger age, children can begin to take some responsibilities. Perhaps it's their job to set the table for lunch, to put away toys (with help), to hang up their clothes (they'll forget now and then), to dress themselves (mostly, that is), to help take care of pets. They should get accustomed to going alone somewhere on an errand—to the corner store, perhaps—or to take a cake down the road to Mr. Brown, who's been ill. It's exciting to spend a night away from home at a friend's house, too, and to learn not to be afraid in a strange bed late at night.

At home both Father and Mother help a child understand his daytime adventures. They explain what he sees and hears, they help him gradually sort out his experiences and find new meanings in them. Facts galore about worlds both real and fancied come to him from the radio and screen. He needs a chance also, to listen to grownups talk; they use words and say things he doesn't quite understand and he asks many, many questions. The best preparation for schoolbooks is a home where there are shelves of stories that Mother and Father obviously treasure. There are wonders inside them all. Someday he too will be able to read quickly and easily like Father and Mother. This provides the incentive to notice letters and find out how his name looks in print. Let's hope there's music, too; he has favorite records which he knows by the pattern on their seals; he learns how to start them playing. He and Mother sing lots of songs together and sometimes they dance. With both parents, even young children can play games of chance and games of skill. One mustn't cheat, they learn (though of course sometimes a small child does); and you have to stick to rules. His father and mother always do.

All this knowledge, all this adventuring help prepare him for school and the beginnings of more formal learning. Even after school days begin parents can still offer mental stimulation at home. Their interest in school life adds to his acceptance of it. When parents and teachers meet and like each other, when home and school pull together, a child is aware of it. Each believes in the other, he discovers, and this fact strengthens his esteem for both. At peace with his home, he will be at peace in school, his mind free for the business of learning.

FIRST DAY,
FIRST GRADE

For as far back as David can remember he has longed for the day when he could go to school. When big brother John started going it was even harder for David to wait, but now the day for him to enter the first grade is drawing near. Whenever he passes the schoolhouse, and long before school is due to open, David can't resist dashing up the steps for another peek through the doors that soon will open for him. Going to school is beginning to seem real and almost too good to be true.

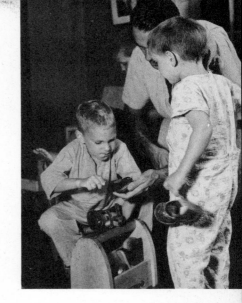

The evening before the great day, Dad helps David get ready. Clothes are laid out, he shines his shoes—is even willing to slick up his brother's shoes. But it's hard to go to sleep and David finds that for all the intensity of his joy there is a slight tinge of other feelings too. Will he be lonely? Will the teacher be nice?

At ten o'clock his parents hear a sound on the stairs, and there's David. The cat can't go to sleep, he says. Mother takes him back upstairs again and a little later, with an old toy and a new lunch box beside him for comfort, David falls into the deep sleep of healthy childhood.

Morning: With time to spare and then some, David's in a tearing hurry over his breakfast. Mother realizes he may really be too excited to eat and doesn't urge him. His full lunch box will come to the rescue later on. The bus is a little late and David's in a tizzy, but he finally sees it coming up the street.

Now he's off, hot on the heels of John and with never a backward glance. Who would ever guess that his tummy's doing all sorts of gyrations? His mother, who is watching from the doorstep, knows very well what's going on under that brave front. He looks little and pathetic. But he'll be all right, she tells herself.

Still whistling to keep up his courage, David yells loudest, waves hardest as the bus approaches. He wants to show the other children he's a regular guy. But in the bus he finds sitting quiet isn't easy. The mirror reflects a tense little face.

28

It's the same steps and the same school building. But David is different. The place
is teeming with strange children who all know each other. Only David is quite
alone. Now he just can't make himself climb those steps and stands sucking his
thumb like a two-year-old.

David at last did find his
courage again and presently
meets Mrs. Donovan, his
teacher. What a relief!
She's lovely. She helps David
print his name. He sits next
to Jeffrey, his old friend.

After a while he looks all around him—out the window, at the pictures on the wall, at what Mrs. Donovan has written on the blackboard. He doesn't quite dare to look as hard at the other children as he might like. Presently Mrs. Donovan asks the whole class to get up and stretch and wiggle their fingers.

It's lunch time, and suddenly he finds himself next to Jeanne. She has blue eyes and yellow braids tied with pink bows. David thinks he never saw anyone so pretty.

At recess he gets terribly embarrassed when he's chosen to be "it" in blindman's buff—stands stock-still, feeling very foolish. How can he guess when he doesn't know anyone's name?

He's glad to be back in the sunshine of Mrs. Donovan's smile again. She pastes a gold star in his workbook. "That was very nice, David," she says.

The classroom is warm and all the children are getting tired and restless at the end of this first exciting day. Even with Jeanne beside him David can't help yawning, and presently both their heads go down on their desks. Just before they leave, brother John comes to visit in David's classroom. Suddenly awake, David shows him around as though he's been there a year.

29

As he leaves school and starts home again. David knows that life's wonderful. His nice teacher makes everything all right. *"And I liked Jeanne best because she's pretty,"* he'll tell his mother later. *He's a real schoolboy at last!*

PHOTOGRAPHER'S NOTE

After you have looked at these picture stories, you may wonder how and under what conditions these photographs were taken. Are they posed or candid? Are these professional models? No, they are not; they are real parents and children in real situations. Nor are they "problem children"; they are just average families who have tried to work out their difficulties in their own way. Finding these families is one of the most important parts of my work and in some cases the most time-consuming one too. Sometimes I just chance upon an interesting situation; in any case, knowing what to look for is half the battle, and after finding a home where a child is actually going through one of these phases, the picture taking is relatively easy.

I should like to emphasize how important it is to try to photograph as if "there were no photographer there at all." If I made friends with the children, the pictures might suffer in truthfulness. For instance, if my presence were to comfort a frightened child, he would no longer desperately want his mother to be there and the point of the picture story would be lost. So a certain friendly aloofness, little if any talk, and great concentration on the child's feelings are absolutely essential in getting such picture stories.

My equipment, or the lack of it, must help me to be as inconspicuous as possible. I use whatever daylight is available, augmented by photofloods or electronic flash reflected from walls or ceiling when necessary. No hot lights, no tripod—in short, a minimum of preoccupation with mechanical things while I am photographing. I use a Rolleiflex almost exclusively for this kind of work; one type of film: Kodak XX; one strong developer, Kodak D 76, for indoor pictures, so I can shoot fast even in poor light; and a milder developer, Kodak Microdol, for outdoor pictures. And, to get back to more essential considerations, I interfere as little as possible with regular routines, personal preferences, and natural moods. I always expect the unexpected to happen; this may take time and patience, but it pays off in results and in the fact that my models have remained my friends. Some of them have become ardent amateur photographers and all firmly believe that pictures taken under the circumstances I just described can serve as valuable aids to a better understanding of their children.

I have changed nothing about the families I photographed, although it is true that in most cases I found it necessary to ignore the existence of other brothers and sisters for purposes of clarity. The children's first names are their own, even though now you may be confused at first about which Johnny is which, and whether the three Davids are one and the same child. (They are not.)

Before I embarked on this series of picture stories, I read many books on the subject and had long conversations with Mrs. Wolf; I spent hours in children's playgrounds, spoke to dozens of mothers on their problems, and watched the children, fascinated by the everyday dramas they enacted. Although technique is necessary, learning as much as possible from and about my subjects was, I think, indispensable for producing these picture stories.

SUZANNE SZASZ

OTHER BOOKS
FOR PARENTS

THE EARLY YEARS

THE COMMON SENSE BOOK OF BABY AND CHILD CARE, by Benjamin Spock, M.D. (527 pages), N.Y.: Duell, Sloan & Pearce, Inc., 1946, $4.00. (Available in a 35-cent edition published by Pocket Books, Inc., as THE POCKET BOOK OF BABY AND CHILD CARE.) An outstanding and comprehensive handbook on baby care by a pediatrician who understands the physical and emotional needs of babies and their families.

INFANT AND CHILD IN THE CULTURE OF TODAY: THE GUIDANCE OF DEVELOPMENT IN HOME AND NURSERY SCHOOL, by Arnold Gesell, M.D., and Frances L. Ilg, M.D. (399 pages), N.Y.: Harper & Brothers, 1943, $4.50. A detailed scientific account of the development of children from infancy to five years.

THE NURSERY YEARS, by Susan Isaacs (138 pages), N.Y.: Vanguard Press, 1937, $2.00. A deep-seeing interpretation of the behavior of young children in the light of their physical, intellectual, and emotional development, with concrete advice on home management.

THE PARENTS' MANUAL: A GUIDE TO THE EMOTIONAL DEVELOPMENT OF YOUNG CHILDREN, by Anna W. M. Wolf (331 pages), N. Y.: Simon and Schuster, Inc., rev. ed. 1951, $3.50. The management of children discussed in warm human terms, to help parents understand themselves and their children and the deeper needs behind everyday behavior.

WHAT TO DO WITH YOUR PRESCHOOLER, by Lillian and Godfrey Frankel (120 pages), N.Y.: Sterling Publishing Co., Inc., 1953, $2.00. Excellent ideas for having fun at home or on trips with children from two to five, based on an understanding of their needs.

THE WONDERFUL STORY OF HOW YOU WERE BORN, by Sidonie Matsner Gruenberg (39 pages), N.Y.: Hanover House, 1952, $2.00. A simple story, beautifully told, to be read aloud to a young child, yet for older children too. A valuable "Guide to Parents" inside the jacket helps parents to put this book to the best possible use.

BROTHERS AND SISTERS, by Edith G. Neisser (241 pages), N.Y.: Harper & Brothers, 1951, $3.00. Warm, simple, and competent discussion of the friction and jealousy to be found in normal children in the same family and of constructive ways of handling the problem. Includes a chapter on twins.

FAMILY LIFE

DEMOCRACY IN THE HOME, by Christine Beasley (242 pages), N.Y.: Association Press, 1954, $3.50. An interesting approach to the field of family relations through the application of the basic principles of democracy to everyday family living.

THE ENCYCLOPEDIA OF CHILD CARE AND GUIDANCE, edited by Sidonie Matsner Gruenberg (1016 pages), N.Y.: Doubleday & Company, Inc., 1954, $7.50. In clear, non-technical language this comprehensive volume covers all phases—physical, psychological, emotional, and educational—from before birth through adolescence. More than 1000 original entries, arranged alphabetically, plus 30 chapters on the basic aspects of child development. By leading authorities. Illustrated.

FATHERS ARE PARENTS, TOO: A CONSTRUCTIVE GUIDE TO SUCCESSFUL FATHERHOOD, by O. Spurgeon English, M.D., and Constance J. Foster (304 pages), N.Y.: G. P. Putnam's Sons, 1951, $3.75. A readable, non-technical explanation of child development and family relations based on psychoanalytic concepts, which stresses the father's contribution to the emotional health of all the family members.

OUR CHILDREN TODAY: A GUIDE TO THEIR NEEDS FROM INFANCY THROUGH ADOLESCENCE, edited by Sidonie M. Gruenberg and the Staff of the Child Study Association of America (366 pages), N. Y.: Viking Press, 1952, $3.95. Twenty-six articles by leaders in education, psychiatry, and allied fields offer parents a stimulating interpretation of new findings in many phases of child development.

THE HAPPY FAMILY, by John Levy, M.D., and Ruth Monroe (319 pages), N.Y.: Alfred A. Knopf, Inc., 1938, $3.50. Problems of marital adjustment and family living, discussed with unusual insight.

PARENTS' QUESTIONS, by the Staff of the Child Study Association of America (256 pages), N.Y.: Harper & Brothers, rev. ed. 1947, $3.00. Everyday questions of parents are met with answers that offer practical advice as well as increased insight into the meaning of behavior.

THE SUBSTANCE OF MENTAL HEALTH, by George H. Preston, M.D. (147 pages), N.Y.: Rinehart & Company, Inc., 1943, $2.50. A clear presentation of the basic laws of mental health and emotional adjustment, informal and reassuring.

THE NURSERY SCHOOL: A HUMAN RELATIONS LABORATORY, by Katherine H. Read (264 pages), Philadelphia: W. B. Saunders Co., 1950, $3.75. A revealing book for parents and teachers, which describes the role of the nursery school in the life of the growing child and stresses its use as a laboratory for the study of human behavior.

SPECIAL SUBJECTS

THE HANDICAPPED CHILD, by Edith M. Stern with Elsa Castendyck (179 pages), N.Y.: A. A. Wyn, Inc., 1950, $2.50. An understanding and informative guide that stresses the importance of sound parental attitudes in meeting the special emotional needs of children with various handicaps.

TELEVISION AND OUR CHILDREN, by Robert Lewis Shayon (94 pages), N.Y.: Longmans, Green & Co., Inc., 1951, $1.75. Surveys the problems raised by TV in relation to children and suggests ways in which parents and the community may meet these

THERE'S MUSIC IN CHILDREN, by Emma Dickson Sheehy (152 pages), N.Y.: Henry Holt & Co., Inc., rev. ed. 1952, $3.00. A gifted teacher explores many ways for creating a favorable musical environment for children to learn and to love music at home and at school.

TODAY'S CHILDREN AND YESTERDAY'S HERITAGE: A PHILOSOPHY OF CREATIVE RELIGIOUS DEVELOPMENT, by Sophia L. Fahs (224 pages), Boston: Beacon Press, 1952, $3.00. An appealing and useful book about children and their religious development. Non-sectarian in approach, it stresses the role of the parent and teacher in helping the child to develop his own beliefs about himself and the nature of the universe.

YOUR CHILD AND HIS ART: A GUIDE FOR PARENTS, by Viktor Lowenfeld (186 pages), N.Y.: The Macmillan Co., 1954, $6.50. This well-illustrated book should be most helpful in fostering children's creative expression from two years old to fourteen.

YOUR CHILD CAN BE HAPPY IN BED: OVER 200 WAYS CHILDREN CAN ENTERTAIN THEM-SELVES, by Cornelia Stratton Parker, N.Y.: Thomas Y. Crowell Co., 1952, $2.95. Helpful suggestions for entertaining sick children, including book and record lists, prepared with true recognition of children's needs.

YOUR CHILD'S READING TODAY, by Josette Frank (328 pages), N.Y.: Doubleday & Company Inc., 1954, $3.95. An authority in the field of children's reading discusses their needs and tastes from the nursery age to the teens. Extensive annotated lists of the best books to be had.

HOW TO BE A WOMAN, by Lawrence K. and Mary Frank (144 pages), Indianapolis: The Bobbs-Merrill Company, Inc., 1954, $2.75. (Also a Maco book, 75 cents.) A thoughtful, down-to-earth consideration of woman's problems today as wife, as mother, as part of the community and, above all, as a human being.

HOW TO HELP THE SHUT-IN CHILD: 313 HINTS FOR HOMEBOUND CHILDREN, by Margery D. McMullin (192 pages), N.Y.: E. P. Dutton & Co., Inc., 1954, $2.75. Over three hundred imaginative and practical games, hobbies, activities, and entertainments for use with the bedridden or homebound child.

We wish to thank the Parents' Book Committee of the Child Study Association of America for permission to use these selections from its book lists.

INDEX

300

DATE D